THE ART OF COOKING
RECIPES & TECHNIQUES

Cooking Arts Collection™

About the Author

Ethel Hofman is a cookbook author, editor, syndicated columnist and culinary consultant to major corporations. She is a past-president of the International Association of Culinary Professionals, a member of the prestigious Les Dames D'Escoffier and was awarded a Doctorate of Food Service from NAFEM (National American Association of Food Equipment Manufacturers).

THE ART OF COOKING: RECIPES & TECHNIQUES

Printed in 2009.

Tom Carpenter, Creative Director

Jennifer Weaverling, Managing Editor

Tad Ware & Company, Inc.,   Contributing Design
Photography
Food Styling
Recipe Testing

Zachary Marell, Design and Production

Bill Lindner Photography, Contributing Photography

On Cover: Aunt Hanni's Blueberry Torte, page 172.

On Page 1: Pork Chops with Dried Apple Stuffing, page 93.

7 8 9 10 11 12 / 13 12 11 10 09
© 2001 Cooking Club of America
ISBN 10: 1-58159-140-3
ISBN 13: 978-1-58159-140-8

Special thanks to: Bill Lindner;
Denise Bornhausen; Mike Hehner;
Steve Schenten; Kay Wethern;
and Kitchen Window, Minneapolis.

Cooking Club of America
12301 Whitewater Drive
Minnetonka, MN 55343
www.cookingclub.com

$\mathcal{T}$ABLE OF CONTENTS

*M*ore than anything else, the passion and pastime of cooking is an art.

Sure, there's some science involved: Working to get fresh, wholesome and suitable ingredients for your creations. Measuring things just right—from how much of an ingredient you use, to setting the cooking temperature just so. Using appropriate tools in the proper way. Really understanding how various cooking techniques work.

These elements are important. But without passion, without ideas, without some creativity and flair, cooking is just a chore. And that's no fun.

That's why we created *The Art of Cooking: Recipes & Techniques* especially and exclusively for you, a valued Cooking Club of America member.

The Art of Cooking combines the elements of cooking (ingredients, tools and skills) with the ideas of cooking (recipes and all their great variations) to generate the creative inspiration you need to become an even better, even more successful, even more accomplished cook.

THE ELEMENTS OF COOKING

We start with the elements of cooking—ingredients, tools and techniques.

First, you'll see how to optimally and efficiently stock your kitchen with ingredients that will range far and wide in your cooking. An organized plan, in conjunction with a well-stocked pantry, refrigerator and freezer,  will free up your time and mind to actually let you concentrate on what's fun—the cooking—and not running around looking for essential ingredients.

Then we'll walk you through a detailed tour of all the tools of cooking—helping you learn even more about their proper usage so you can put them to work efficiently and effectively in your own cooking.

And you'll learn cooking skills. You may already know some of them. But guaranteed, some will be new to you. Either way, this area of "skills" is where you bring the ingredients and tools together. You'll understand cooking better, gleaning knowledge you can put to work right away.

THE IDEAS OF COOKING

Of course, we're not going to present all that great information and then leave you to fend for yourself. Ingredients, tools and skills meld together through recipes, and that's where we take you next, with 12 idea-filled chapters on everything from appetizers to dessert and most everything in between.

In all, you'll find dozens upon dozens of recipes, with multiple variations in many cases, in the following categories:

Appetizers & Snacks	**Poultry**
Breads	**Salads**
Breakfast & Brunch	**Sandwiches**
Fish & Seafood	**Side Dishes**
Meat	**Soups**
Pasta	**Desserts**

Each of these chapters offers a wide variety of both "Essential" and "Master" recipes. The essential recipes are ideas every cook should have; they also present building blocks you can use as the bases for your own new recipes and creations. The master recipes take ingredients and skills a step or two farther, presenting more advanced and challenging ideas that will be new and valuable to your recipe repertoire.

But there is much more than just an ingredient list and set of instructions with each recipe.

Cooking tips present themselves where a particular technique or idea, specific to the recipe at hand, is needed. Nutritional information is included for each dish, as is a preparation timeline so you can manage your work. You'll find plenty of variations on many of the recipes, each one essentially creating a whole new taste and a whole new recipe! We've included chef's notes as well, outlining important techniques and cooking advice.

THE ART OF COOKING

If cooking were simple and mundane, it wouldn't be so exciting or interesting. The challenge of making something great, the creativity of trying new things, the rewards of serving (and tasting for yourself) the successful dishes you've prepared … these are the ideas that make cooking an art.

And cooking truly is an art—a passion and pastime to be savored both in the kitchen as well as at the table. *The Art of Cooking* will help you become even more successful on your own personal cooking journey.

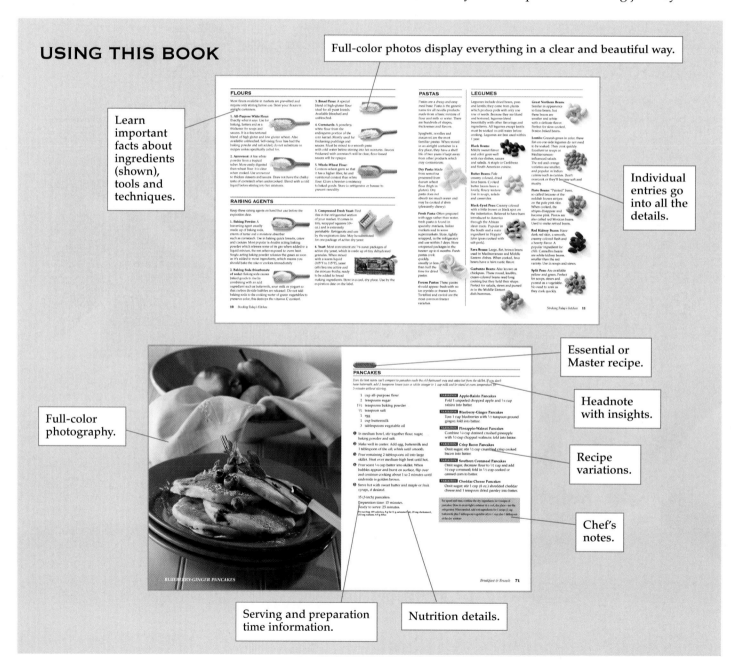

USING THIS BOOK

Full-color photos display everything in a clear and beautiful way.

Learn important facts about ingredients (shown), tools and techniques.

Individual entries go into all the details.

Full-color photography.

Essential or Master recipe.

Headnote with insights.

Recipe variations.

Chef's notes.

Serving and preparation time information.

Nutrition details.

STOCKING TODAY'S KITCHEN

Great cooking starts with great ingredients. With the organized lists, easy-to-follow guidelines and comprehensive plans presented here, you'll be able to stock your kitchen with the items you'll need to operate efficiently and effectively.

INGREDIENTS: Stocking Today's Kitchen

Cooking today has taken on new meaning. Just walk into a supermarket to see ingredients that were either expensive or unobtainable a decade ago that are now easily within consumers' budgets. Fresh vegetables, peeled and washed, are ready to pour from a bag to cook and serve. Fruits such as strawberries are now available year-round, shipped in from California or South America. And there's an extraordinary variety of rubs, marinades and dressings to intensify the flavors of sweet and savory dishes.

I love to cook. Happily, my husband Walter and our family and friends all love to eat. Our meals are well-balanced, delicious and in keeping with a busy lifestyle. How? I've created a style of home-cooking without the hassle of long ingredient lists and with techniques that are simple when fully explained. It all begins with a well-organized pantry stocked with the basics, the frequently used items and your own favorite ingredients. Here are the details.

PANTRY PLANNING AND ORGANIZATION

Here are a few guidelines on organizing your pantry for maximum efficiency.

- The pantry should be cool, dry and clean.

- Line shelves with shelving paper with adhesive backing. Wipe with a damp cloth. Let dry thoroughly before arranging items on shelves. If shelves are wire-plastic coated, wipe thoroughly and allow to dry.

- Place seldom used items on the top shelves.

- Teas, coffee, breakfast cereals and other basics should be easy to reach.

- Arrange similar items together: Unopened oils, vinegars and other condiments. Put canned fruits and vegetables in one area.

- Legumes (dried peas, beans and lentils) are cheaper than canned and take up less storage space.

- Check your supplies every 2 to 3 months, replacing ingredients as needed. Flours should be used within 2 months, so buy small quantities unless you plan to do a lot of baking at holiday times. Most flours are pre-sifted so that you need only stir and then spoon into a measuring cup.

SUGARS

There are endless uses for sugar in the kitchen. Use it for sweetener as well as a tenderizer for doughs.

1. Brown Sugar:
White sugar mixed with refined molasses, which helps give it a soft texture. It is available as  dark and light. Generally, the lighter in color, the more delicate the flavor. Brown sugar tends to harden if not tightly sealed. If stored in the freezer, sugar will soften in a few minutes at room temperature. Or soften by adding a thick apple wedge, cut side up, on top of sugar in a microwave dish. Cover with vented plastic wrap and microwave on High for 30 to 60 seconds until softened. Let stand 1 minute. Stir.

2. Confectioner's Sugar:
Granulated sugar that has been crushed to a fine powder. A very small  amount of cornstarch (less than 3%) is added to keep it free-flowing but is best sifted as needed. Use for frostings and icings, and to sift over cakes and desserts to decorate.

3. Granulated Sugar: A white all-purpose sugar. Superfine sugar (castor sugar) is more finely  granulated so that it dissolves more quickly in items such as cold drinks and in meringues.

4. Raw Sugar: Grainy brown sugar. It is the residue left after the sugar cane has been processed to remove  the molasses. Sweetens coffee and teas or sprinkle over cookies before baking.

SWEETENERS

Sweeteners are used as flavoring agents in baked goods, and for many other purposes.

1. Corn Syrup: Available light and dark. A sweet syrup prepared by processing corn sugar with acids or enzymes. It does not crystallize. Use in pecan pie, frostings, candy, jams and jellies.

2. Honey: A clear, sweet, runny liquid gathered by bees from flower nectars such as heather, buckwheat and orange blossom. Honey is extracted from the comb and may be pasteurized to help prevent crystallization. Comb honey is the chewy comb containing the liquid honey—all of which may be eaten.

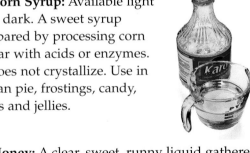

3. Maple Syrup: Thick and syrupy from the boiled-down sap of the maple tree. Delicious poured over pancakes and waffles. The real thing!

4. Molasses: The mixture left after sugar crystals have been extracted from the sugar cane and sugar beets. A distinctively flavored, thick, light or dark syrup. Use in American regional dishes like gingerbread, Indian pudding and Boston baked beans.

FLOURS

Most flours available in markets are pre-sifted and require only stirring before use. Store your flours in airtight containers.

1. All-Purpose White Flour:
Exactly what it says. Use for baking, batters and as a thickener for soups and sauces. It is a fine textured  blend of high gluten and low gluten wheat. Also available unbleached. Self-rising flour has had the baking powder and salt added; do not substitute in recipes unless specifically called for.

2. Arrowroot: A fine white powder from a tropical tuber. More easily digested than wheat flour. It is clear when cooked. Use arrowroot to thicken desserts and sauces. Does not have the chalky taste of cornstarch when undercooked. Blend with a cold liquid before stirring into hot mixtures.

3. Bread Flour: A special blend of high-gluten flour ideal for all yeast breads. Available bleached and unbleached.

4. Cornstarch: A powdery, white flour from the endosperm portion of the corn kernel. Mostly used for thickening puddings and  sauces. Must be mixed to a smooth paste with cold water before stirring into hot mixtures. Sauces thickened with cornstarch will be clear; flour-based sauces will be opaque.

5. Whole-Wheat Flour:
Contains wheat germ so that it has a higher fiber, fat and nutritional content than white flour. Gives a heavier consistency to baked goods. Store in refrigerator or freezer to prevent rancidity.

RAISING AGENTS

Keep these raising agents on hand but use before the expiration date.

1. Baking Powder: A leavening agent usually made up of baking soda, 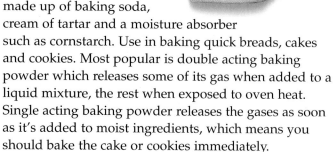 cream of tartar and a moisture absorber such as cornstarch. Use in baking quick breads, cakes and cookies. Most popular is double acting baking powder which releases some of its gas when added to a liquid mixture, the rest when exposed to oven heat. Single acting baking powder releases the gases as soon as it's added to moist ingredients, which means you should bake the cake or cookies immediately.

2. Baking Soda (bicarbonate of soda): Baking soda causes baked goods to rise by combining with an acid  ingredient such as buttermilk, sour milk or yogurt so that carbon dioxide bubbles are released. Do not add baking soda to the cooking water of green vegetables to preserve color; this destroys the vitamin C content.

3. Compressed Fresh Yeast: Find this in the refrigerated section of your market. It comes in tiny, wrapped squares (.06-oz.) and is extremely perishable. Refrigerate and use by the expiration date. May be substituted for one package of active dry yeast.

4. Yeast: Most convenient are 1/4-ounce packages of active dry yeast, which is made up of tiny dehydrated granules. When mixed with a warm liquid (105°F to 115°F), yeast  cells become active and the mixture frothy, ready to be added to bread making ingredients. Store in a cool, dry place. Use by the expiration date on the label.

PASTAS

Pastas are a cheap and easy meal base. Pasta is the generic name for all noodle products made from a basic mixture of flour and milk or water. There are hundreds of shapes, thicknesses and flavors.

Spaghetti, noodles and macaroni are the most familiar pastas. When stored in an airtight container in a dry place, they have a shelf life of two years if kept away from other products which may contaminate.

Dry Pasta: Made from semolina processed from durum wheat flour (high in gluten). Dry pasta does not absorb too much water and may be cooked *al dente* (pleasantly chewy).

Fresh Pasta: Often prepared with eggs rather than water, fresh pasta is found in specialty markets, Italian markets and in some supermarkets. Store, tightly wrapped, in the refrigerator and use within 3 days. Store unopened packages in the freezer up to 6 months. Fresh pastas cook quickly, usually in less than half the time for dried pastas.

Frozen Pastas: These pastas should appear fresh with no ice crystals or freezer burn. Tortellini and ravioli are the most common freezer varieties.

LEGUMES

Legumes include dried beans, peas and lentils; they come from plants which produce pods with only one row of seeds. Because they are bland and textured, legumes blend beautifully with other flavorings and ingredients. All legumes except lentils must be soaked in cold water before cooking. Legumes are best used within 1 year.

Black Beans: Mildly sweet flavor and color goes well with rice dishes, sauces and salads. A staple in Caribbean and South American cuisine.

Butter Beans: Pale creamy colored, dried lima beans. Cooked butter beans have a lovely, floury texture. Use in soups, salads and casseroles.

Black-Eyed Peas: Creamy colored with a little brown or black spot on the indentation. Believed to have been introduced to America through the African slave trade. Popular in the South and a main ingredient in Hoppin' John (peas cooked with salt pork).

Fava Beans: Large, flat, brown beans used in Mediterranean and Middle Eastern dishes. When cooked, fava beans have a faint rustic flavor.

Garbanzo Beans: Also known as chickpeas. These round, knobby, cream-colored beans need long cooking but they hold their shape. Perfect for salads, stews and pureed as in the Middle Eastern dish hummus.

Great Northern Beans: Similar in appearance to lima beans, but these beans are smaller and white with a delicate flavor. Perfect for slow-cooked, Boston baked beans.

Lentils: Grayish-green in color, these flat-on-one-side legumes do not need to be soaked. They cook quickly. Excellent in soups or Mediterranean-influenced salads. The red and orange varieties are smaller, and popular in Indian cuisine such as curries. Don't overcook or they'll become soft and mushy.

Pinto Beans: "Painted" bean, so called because of the reddish brown stripes on the pale pink skin. When cooked, the stripes disappear and become pink. Pintos are also called red Mexican beans. Used to make refried beans.

Red Kidney Beans: Have dark red skin, a smooth, creamy colored flesh and a hearty flavor. A popular ingredient for chili. Cannellini beans are white kidney beans, smaller than the red variety. Use in soups and stews.

Split Peas: Are available yellow and green. Perfect for soups, stews and pureed as a vegetable. No need to soak as they cook quickly.

GRAINS

Grains are cheap international staples that are high in fiber, low in fat and have zero cholesterol. They include any plant from the grass family that yields an edible seed. Most familiar are rice, barley, corn, oats, bulgur and cornmeal. Store grains in a cool, dry place. Most grains may be stored indefinitely but are best used within a year.

Barley: One of the oldest grains. Hulled barley is the most nutritious because only the outer husk has been removed. Most popular is pearl barley where the bran and outer husk is removed, and kernels are polished and white.

Bulgur: Steamed, dried and hulled cracked wheat. A Middle Eastern staple used in dishes such as tabbouleh (bulgur and vegetable salad) and pilafs.

Cornmeal: Prepared from dried corn kernels and available in fine, medium and coarse textures. Cornmeal may be yellow, white or blue, depending on the type of corn used. Cornmeal is the main ingredient in polenta (a porridge-like mixture), an Italian staple eaten hot with butter or grated cheese.

Couscous: Often thought of as a grain but really a type of pasta. Packaged instant couscous, prepared in 5 minutes, is one of the easiest and fastest side dishes you can serve.

Grits: Coarsely ground grain similar to cornmeal. Available ground coarse, medium or fine. Cooked with milk or water, grits can be eaten as a hot cereal or with a pat of butter as a side dish.

Kasha (buckwheat groats): Whole or coarse roasted buckwheat kernels with a nutty, chewy flavor and texture. Widely used in eastern European cooking.

Quinoa (keenwa): An ancient grain still popular in South American dishes. Quinoa is higher in protein than any other grain and is considered a complete protein since it contains the eight essential amino acids. The tiny, cream-colored beads cook more quickly than rice. Available in health food stores and most supermarkets.

Rice: A staple food in China, India and Southeast Asia but popular across the world now. Here are some of the most popular rice varieties:

- *Arborio Rice:* Grains are short and fat with a high starch content. Excellent for risotto (a creamy rice dish) and paella (saffron flavored rice and seafood dish).

- *Basmati Rice:* A long-grain, exotic, perfumy rice. When cooked, the grains are light, dry and separate easily.

- *Brown Rice:* The entire grain of rice with only the outer hull removed. This is a high fiber, nutritious grain with a nutty flavor. Brown rice takes longer to cook than long grain rice, but it's also available as instant. Because of the bran, brown rice may become rancid. Store in a cool, dry place and use within 6 months.

- *Long Grain:* An excellent all-purpose rice, usually enriched, which has been processed to remove the hull, germ and most of the bran. It is also available in instant (commercially cooked) and dehydrated forms.

- *Wild Rice:* Really the seeds of a long-grain marsh grass grown in the northern Great Lakes area but now commercially grown in other states including California and the Midwest. This expensive grain takes a long time to cook, often up to 1 hour.

Wheat Germ: Tiny golden-colored crunchy grains with a nutty flavor. No need to cook. Sprinkle over cereals, breads and muffins before baking.

Wheat Berries: Unprocessed wheat kernels. Must be presoaked. Use a long cooking time to tenderize. Toss with dried cranberries for a deliciously chewy salad.

HERBS AND LEAVES

Herbs have been treasured for centuries. Besides making foods more appealing, herbs have been used to crown royalty, as medicines, and have been found in burial tombs.

Basil: A refreshing combination of cloves and mint. Fresh basil is best. If using dried basil, use within 3 months. Basil is a perfect enhancement for fresh tomatoes, tomato and cheese dishes, and Italian sauces.

Marjoram: Oval, pale-green leaves with a mild, sweet taste. Available dried and crumbled. Especially good to flavor lamb, veal, poultry and vegetables.

Oregano: A strong, mint-like flavored herb to be used sparingly. Usually dried and crumbled. Use oregano in tomato based dishes such as lasagna or pizza topping.

Rosemary: Easily recognized by thin, dark green, spiky, needle-like leaves. The fresh citrus and pine flavors and aromas go well with lamb, fish and egg dishes. The dried variety is milder than the fresh.

Sage: Dusty green leaves and a musty aroma, but a pleasant, mint flavor. Dried sage comes crumbled and ground. Use sage to flavor pork, poultry, sausages and stuffing.

Bay Leaves: An aromatic Mediterranean herb from the laurel tree. Available dried. The Turkish variety has a more delicate flavor than the Californian. Use in soups and stews. Only one or two bay leaves are needed for each dish. Remove before serving.

SEEDS

Purchase spice seeds whole. Do not grind seeds until you are ready to use them. The flavor of seeds is enhanced by toasting one or two minutes in a dry skillet.

Anise Seed: Has a licorice-like flavor and is used in Asian cooking, for aromatic sweets and for savory dishes. This is the flavoring in drinks such as anisette and ouzo. Star anise is a dark brown pod containing tiny seeds with a faintly bitter taste. Anise is one of the ingredients in Chinese Five-Spice powder.

Caraway Seeds: Have a strong anise flavor, which is an acquired taste. Widely used in German and Hungarian cooking. Use to flavor cheeses, rye breads, sausages and cabbage dishes.

Dill Seeds: Flat and pale brown with creamy edges. Used mainly for the brine for dill pickles. Toast dill lightly before using to intensify the flavor.

Fennel Seeds: Are oval and greenish brown in color. Licorice flavor similar to anise. Use in savory dishes such as seafood dishes, borscht and Italian breads.

Mustard Seeds: Most common are the pungent, brown variety used for pickling vegetables and as the main ingredient in Chinese mustard. White mustard seeds are larger than the brown, less pungent, and one of the ingredients in yellow, mild American-style mustards.

Poppy Seeds: Tiny, bluish-black, crunchy seeds from the poppy plant. Poppy seeds are crunchy and nutty flavored. Used as a filling for coffee cakes and pastries, tossed in with noodles, as a topping and in salad dressings.

Sesame Seeds (also called benne): Tiny, flat, pale brown seeds with a sweet, nutty flavor and high oil content. To prevent rancidity, store in an airtight jar in a cool, dry place up to 3 months, or in the freezer for up to a year. Used in Middle Eastern delicacies such as halvah (a sesame candy), and in cakes and cookies.

SPICES

Use spices to enhance a variety of foods, both sweet and savory. Whole spices such as nutmeg may be ground in a mortar and pestle or spice grinder as needed. Ground spices quickly lose their flavor so buy only your favorites. Buy in small quantities and store in tight-lidded containers in a cool, dry place or in resealable plastic bags in the freezer. Use within 6 months, or up to a year if the spices were stored in the freezer.

Allspice: A small berry from the evergreen pimiento tree in the West Indies and South America. Taste is a combination of cinnamon, nutmeg and cloves. Use in sweet and savory dishes.

Cardamom: A member of the ginger family but with a more delicate floral aroma. Use in Scandinavian and East Indian cooking. Purchase in the pods or ground. Use cardamom sparingly in coffee cakes, Danish pastries, stews and curries.

Cinnamon: Possibly the most widely used spice. Cinnamon comes from the bark of a tropical tree and is most often used ground. Cinnamon sticks are used as a "stirrer" for hot drinks and to infuse syrups and liquids. The powder is slightly bittersweet and packs a pleasing punch when added to desserts and baked goods.

Cloves: The dried, unopened bud of the tropical clove tree. A clove looks like a dark brown nail, and is strongly flavored and very pungent. Available whole and ground. Use cloves to stud oranges, stew onions and bake hams. Try in sweet breads, coffee cakes, and lightly in savory dishes such as stews.

Coriander (cilantro): Similar in appearance to flat leaf parsley but quite a different flavor. Available in seeds or ground, or fresh as leaves. The seeds have a citrus-sage aroma. Use to flavor pickles and mulled wines. Ground coriander is a favorite Scandinavian flavoring for baked items. Delicious in rice dishes, soups and salads but don't use unless you know your guests like it.

Cumin: Similar in shape to a caraway seed. Available in ground or seeds forms, cumin is an essential flavoring in Middle Eastern dishes. Cumin is one of the main flavorings in Kummel, a sweet, clear liqueur.

Ginger: From a tropical plant with a thin-skinned, bumpy root. Ground ginger is aromatic and spicy. Use it in baked items and in Asian cooking. Ginger is also available fresh. Store unpeeled, wrapped tightly in plastic wrap and refrigerate up to 10 days. Do not substitute in recipes calling for ground ginger. Use fresh ginger in curries, meat dishes and fruit compotes.

Mace: The lacy covering of the nutmeg seed. When ground and dried, mace is deep orange, with incredibly intense nutmeg flavor. Mace is often available in long, thin pieces called "blades."

Nutmeg: The seed of the nutmeg tree. Nutmeg yields a warm, spicy-sweet flavor. Sold both ground and whole. Grated whole nutmeg is more flavorful than the ground. Use in milk-based dishes such as custards, eggnog, or to spike vegetable dishes.

Pepper: Used sparingly, most peppers are pungent and fierce tasting. Available as whole peppercorns, ground black and white pepper. Cayenne pepper is a fiery ground red pepper you should only use with caution. Crush dry peppercorns with a pepper mill.

Saffron: The world's priciest spice. Saffron comes from the dried, orange stigmas of a small purple crocus. Use saffron sparingly, to flavor and color foods. Available both in powder and threads; the latter is crushed and added to the dish or soaked in warm water for 15 minutes or so before using the colored liquid. Use metal or plastic cooking utensils, not wood; the wood will absorb some of your precious, costly saffron.

Salt: Comes in several forms. Table salt is a fine-grained salt with additives to make it pour easily. Used in cooking and as a condiment. Iodized salt is table salt with added iodine to help prevent hypothyroidism. Coarse salts, such as kosher salt and rock and sea salts, are used mainly for cooking. Kosher salt is used by observant Jews to prepare meats; some chefs prefer its texture and flavor.

Turmeric: Related to ginger, but with a slightly bitter taste and a deep yellow color. Turmeric is used mainly for adding color to food. A main ingredient in mustard. Also used in curries and Indian cooking.

BLENDED SEASONINGS

Blended seasonings are not only easy, quick and flavor enhancing, but they're also convenient and economical. Buy in small quantities and store in air-tight containers.

Apple Pie Spice: A blend of cinnamon, cloves, nutmeg, allspice and ginger. Use in fruit pies and chutneys.

Chili Powder: Dried ground chilies, garlic, coriander, cumin, oregano, cloves and other pungent spices. Use for chili and stews.

Crab or Shrimp Boil: A blend of whole spices and herbs such as peppercorns, bay leaves, allspice, crushed red peppers and mustard seed. The most popular brand name is Old Bay.

Curry Powder: May be a blend of up to 20 spices and herbs including fennel seed, cumin, saffron and turmeric (which gives curries their characteristic yellow color).

Five-Spice Powder: A blend of aromatic spices including star anise, cinnamon and cloves. Use in Asian cooking.

Herbes de Provence: A blend of crushed dried herbs similar to those used in southern France. Includes basil, sage, thyme, lavender, summer savory and rosemary. Use to season meat, poultry and vegetable dishes.

Herb Seasonings: Many varieties. Blends include dried herbs, salt and peppers. May be mild or pungent. Use to season any savory dish such as a sauce, meat loaf or casserole.

Italian Seasoning: A blend of oregano, basil, sweet red pepper, rosemary and garlic. Use to season meat sauces, lasagna and other Italian dishes.

Lemon-Pepper Seasoning: If you keep this on your shelf there's little need for salt and pepper. Made up of ground black pepper, salt, dried lemon peel and other natural additives.

Poultry Seasoning: An enormous variety to choose from. Usually a blend of sage, thyme, marjoram, savory and other spices.

Pumpkin Pie Spice: A blend of nutmeg, cinnamon and ginger. Other spices to enhance pumpkin dishes may be included.

Tandoori Blend: Indian-influenced spices such as coriander, ginger, cumin, cloves, turmeric and cardamom. Use this blend for Tandoori chicken. "Tandoori" is a clay oven used throughout India.

OILS

Liquid vegetable oils are highly regarded for their flavors, unique cooking properties and nutritional value. Oils such as corn oil and safflower oil are polyunsaturated and are healthier than butter and other animal fats. Most vegetable oils have high smoke points and are a good choice for frying; food may be cooked at a high temperature without burning. Store oils in a cool, dark place. Good quality oils need no refrigeration; but if refrigerated, olive oils may become cloudy. Bring to room temperature and they will clear and pour easily.

Vinegars are one of the best buys in the marketplace. Versatile uses include flavoring, preserving, marinating and tenderizing. The most popular vinegar in the United States is apple cider vinegar, made from fermented cider and distilled white vinegar.

Cold-Pressed, Extra-Virgin Olive Oil: The finest and most expensive olive oil comes from the first pressing of olives. It is fruity flavored and contains extremely low levels of acidity. Perfect for salad dressings, marinades, or as a "dunk" for breads instead of butter. Don't use for frying—it's a waste of money since the flavor breaks down at high heat.

Light Olive Oil: Filtered olive oil that is pale in color, with very little of the classic fruity olive-oil flavor. This makes it ideal for baking, frying and other dishes where a distinct olive flavor is not needed.

Olive Oils: Monounsaturated oils pressed from ripe olives. These oils are graded according to their acid content, and vary in flavor depending on the country of origin.

VINEGARS

A variety of vinegars are available in today's markets. Store vinegar in a cool, dark place. Store opened vinegar 6 months; unopened vinegar can be stored indefinitely.

Balsamic Vinegar: Gets its rich dark color and syrupy sweetness from being aged in wooden barrels. Intensely flavored, use sparingly in salad dressings, and to sprinkle over cooked vegetables.

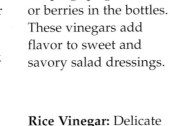

Herb and Fruit Infused Vinegars: Made by steeping sprigs of herbs or berries in the bottles. These vinegars add flavor to sweet and savory salad dressings.

Rice Vinegar: Delicate and sweet, made from fermented rice. A key ingredient in Japanese and Chinese cooking.

Wine Vinegars: Made from red or white wines, which give pungency to dishes such as marinated herring and sauerbraten.

SAUCES

Sauces are instant taste enhancers. Sauces may be sweet or savory, thick or thin. Storage directions vary. Check the labels.

Barbecue Sauce: Not only for barbecued foods, this sauce may be sweet or hot but always full of zesty flavor. Use to brush over meats while cooking, incorporate into a meat loaf mixture, or as an accompaniment for cooked meats and poultry. Traditional ingredients are tomatoes, onions, garlic, vinegars, brown sugar. Other ingredients may be included according to region and brand.

Marinades: Available in pouches you mix, or prepared in jars and bottles. Marinades may be sweet or savory and should be refrigerated after opening. Papaya is a favorite ingredient in marinades, containing an enzyme which helps tenderize meats.

Mint Sauce: A tangy, dark green mixture of chopped fresh mint, vinegar and brown sugar. It is traditionally served with roast lamb. The more popular mint jelly is a mild, sweet condiment served with roast meats, fish and poultry.

Soy Sauce: Prepared from fermented, boiled soy beans. This richly brown salty sauce is a prime ingredient in Asian cooking. Low sodium varieties are also available. Soy sauce is a good marinade ingredient. Also use as flavoring for stir-fried dishes, poultry, fish and vegetables.

Tabasco: Trademarked name held by the McIlhenny family in Louisiana. Hot peppers are fermented before adding to other ingredients to make the sauce. A few drops of Tabasco are often enough to pack a breathtaking punch to bland dishes.

Teriyaki Sauce: A tangy, syrupy mixture usually of soy sauce, sherry, sugar, ginger, sesame seeds and other seasonings depending on the brand. Pour on chicken, fish or steaks before cooking, or use as a marinade. The high sugar content gives a light, sweet glaze on cooking.

Worcestershire Sauce: Thin, dark brown, piquant sauce. It was first produced in Worcester, England, but was developed in India by the English. Worcestershire sauce is used as a table condiment as well as a seasoning for cooked meats and in Bloody Mary cocktails.

MUSTARD

Comes in several varieties and strengths. Mustards should be refrigerated after opening. A multitude of imported and domestic mustards are available in today's markets. Refrigerate opened mustard; store unopened mustard in cool, dark place for no more than 2 years.

Dijon Mustard: Tangy and hot, prepared from brown mustard seeds.

Dry or Powdered Mustard: Made from finely ground mustard seeds. Concentrated and very hot. Use where blending without lumping is important, as in flavored breads.

Salad Mustard: A mild, yellow, smooth mixture containing white mustard seed, vinegar, sugar and turmeric.

CONDIMENTS

Like sauces, condiments are taste enhancers. Readily available in supermarkets, these specific condiments come in a variety of flavors. Condiments can be sweet, savory, chunky or smooth accompaniments to food.

Ketchup: A smooth blend of tomatoes, vinegar and sugar. Use on hamburgers, frankfurters and other fast foods. Ketchup is often a key ingredient in relishes and salsas.

Chutneys: It used to be that Major Grey's was the only brand of chutney available. Now you can choose from a huge number of fruit and vegetable chutneys ranging from mild and sweet to hot and spicy. They may be smooth or chunky, contain fruits or vegetables, vinegar, sugar and spices. Chutney is the usual accompaniment to Indian dishes such as curry, but try as a spread over sandwich fillings, slathered on breads, or spooned over a slab of cream cheese or other cheese.

Salsa: Originally a Mexican sauce, tomato based salsas have become almost as popular as ketchup. Medium thick and chunky, salsas contain peppers, tomatoes and seasonings and come in three degrees of heat: mild, medium and hot.

FLAVORINGS AND RUBS

Flavorings are extracts obtained from various plants or foods. Highly concentrated, flavorings are usually used by the teaspoonful or less.

Blended Seasonings: Mixtures of pungent herbs and spices. When rubbed into the oiled surfaces of poultry, fish and meats, the flavor is better absorbed and more intense than when a seasoning is sprinkled over. Wear gloves so that any strong food odors (such as garlic) are avoided. This is an especially good method for foods cooked on the barbecue.

Bouillon Cubes: Savory extracts obtained from beef, chicken or vegetables. A timesaving substitute for the long process of making stock.

Vanilla and Almond Extract: Most commonly used in baking and for flavoring puddings.

Vanilla Beans: Encased in dried, long, brown pods. Split lengthwise, vanilla beans infuse milk mixtures and custards with a light perfume, or place the beans in a storage jar of sugar to create vanilla-flavored sugar. Excellent to sprinkle on cakes and cookies and in baking. Avoid synthetic flavorings—the aroma and flavors are entirely different.

CANNED FOOD

Canned products are an essential safety net for the homemaker—and there are more than 1,500 items to choose from. Along with the traditional favorites like peaches and tomatoes, each week new specialty foods appear on the supermarket shelves, providing endless possibilities for quick, delicious meals.

In winter, canned fruits, with the addition of diced fresh fruits such as apples and pears, make an almost instant fruit salad. Instead of cooking dried beans and other legumes, canned beans are ready to be combined with other ingredients for a side dish or to add to soups. Canned tuna or chicken is quickly transformed into salads, and fish takes on a mouthwatering flavor and appearance when baked in Italian-style canned tomatoes.

Canned food is packed full of nutrition. In most cases, it is equally nutritious to the fresh and frozen items. And it's available year-round!

Some canned products now have a "for best quality use by" date on the top or bottom of the can. True expiration dates are rarely found on canned food. The general rule is that canned goods have a shelf life of at least two years from the date of processing, but the food keeps its safety and nutritional value well beyond that. Do not buy cans that are dented or bulging.

Your canned food supply is an oversized recipe toolbox. Depending on size of family and personal tastes, quantities and choice of the items in your "Perfect Canned Food Pantry" (following) may vary.

THE PERFECT CANNED FOOD PANTRY
WHAT EVERY PANTRY NEEDS

Fruits:
- peach slices in heavy or lite syrup
- apricot halves in heavy or lite syrup
- fruit cocktail in heavy or lite syrup
- mandarin oranges
- pear halves in heavy or lite syrup
- pineapple chunks in heavy or lite syrup
- pitted cherries (delicious over ice cream)
- dakota figs in syrup
- unsweetened applesauce
- fruit pie filling
- whole cranberry sauce

Vegetables:
- small peeled potatoes
- vacuum packed yams
- whole tomatoes
- Italian-style diced tomatoes
- tomato paste
- tomato sauce
- baby beets
- diced chilies
- sauerkraut
- creamed corn
- corn kernels
- black, red and white beans
- garbanzo beans

Fish, Meats and Miscellaneous:
- tuna
- chicken
- salmon
- minced clams
- evaporated milk
- condensed milk

Nice to Have:
- smoked oysters
- pates
- crabmeat
- anchovies
- artichoke hearts
- snacking nuts
- almond paste
- canned chestnuts in syrup

VEGETABLES

CHOOSING

Whether they're from your garden, your local farmers' market or neighborhood grocery, vegetables taste better fresh. That's why you should purchase them in small quantities and more frequently.

Fresh vegetables are vibrant in color and feel firm. Use your judgement—if it doesn't look or feel fresh, it probably isn't. Keep in mind, vegetables are usually at their best quality and price at the peak of their season.

STORING

Store most vegetables in the refrigerator. The coolness slows down enzyme activity and retains freshness.

Place unwashed vegetables in plastic bags in the vegetable crisper. Lettuces should be washed, spin-dried, placed in a paper-towel-lined plastic bag and refrigerated. Use within 2 days.

Remove the tops of carrots and beets before storing. If the tops are left on, these vegetables will become limp and dry. The exceptions are potatoes, onions and thick-skinned winter squashes. Ideally, these should be stored in a cool, dark, dry place between 55°F and 65°F; they will keep up to 7 weeks. Any potatoes purchased should be firm with no sprouting eyes, soft black spots or green areas; the latter may be slightly toxic.

Use these guidelines for optimal vegetable flavor and freshness.

VEGETABLE	CHOICE	Refrigeration TIME
Asparagus	firm, green stalks with tight buds	1-2 days
Beets	small, firm, dark red	7 days
Bell Peppers	shiny skin, firm, with no signs of decay	3-5 days
Broccoli	dark green, firm stalks with tight buds	1-2 days
Brussel Sprouts	round headed and hard with tight leaves	1-2 days
Cabbage	round headed and hard with tight leaves	1-2 weeks
Carrots	good color, firm and smooth	7 days
Cauliflower	unblemished, cream white, tight florets	3-5 days
Corn on the Cob	green husks with plump kernels	up to 1 day
Cucumber	hard, dark green	3-5 days
Eggplant	glossy, purple, unblemished	1-2 days
Green Wax Beans	bright-colored, crisp, snap when bent	1-2 days
Leeks	green leaves and white bulbous ends	3-5 days
Lettuces	bright-colored, crisp leaves, unwilted	1-2 days
Mushrooms	smooth, unblemished	1-2 days
Okra	green, snap when bent	1-2 days
Parsnips	cream colored, firm with no soft spots	7 days
Peas	round, shiny in bright, green pods	1-2 days
Spinach	bright, crisp leaves with thin stems	1-2 days
Tomatoes	smooth, good color, no soft spots	1-2 days
Turnips	small, white with pinkish area round stems	1-2 weeks
Summer Squash	bright colored, unblemished, firm	3-5 days

FRUITS

CHOOSING

In season, take a drive into the country and look for locally grown fruits, or head to a farmers' market. These fruit items are fresher and tastier then those shipped long distances from larger farms.

And keep in mind that good fruits don't have to be picture perfect. Some of the best fruits may have a lump or bump. Avoid fruit in plastic bags: It's impossible to test the firmness and quality of each piece. Contrary to some shopper's practices, thumping a melon does not indicate ripeness. Rather, feel the product.

In general, fruits that are too soft are too ripe; if too hard, it's not ripe enough. Try the sniff test for certain fruits such as peaches, pears and melons. A strong perfume means they are nicely ripened.

STORING

Cold storage adds to the keeping qualities of fruit after they are harvested.

Ripe fruits should be refrigerated or stored in a cool place. Except for berries and cherries, all fruit should be washed and dried before refrigerating. Pick through berries and cherries, discarding any that are moldy or over-soft. If you don't do this, the remaining berries will spoil quickly.

Melons may be kept at room temperature until they soften. But for fullest flavor, always bring fruits back toward room temperature before eating. It's almost impossible to judge a whole watermelon. Select a piece that is crisp, with rosy red flesh. Many fruits may be ripened at room temperature and then refrigerated.

Use these guidelines for optimal fruit flavor and freshness.

FRUIT	CHOICE	Refrigeration TIME
Apples	smooth skin, firm, unblemished	6 weeks
Apricots	plump, well-formed, fairly firm	3-4 days
Avocado	good green color, yielding to gentle pressure	7 days
Blackberries	plump with good dark color	1 day
Blueberries	large and firm with a dusty bloom	7-10 days
Cherries	firm, plump, green stems	2-3 days
Dates	plump and moist	3-5 days
Grapefruit	smooth skin, plump, heavy	2-3 weeks
Grapes	clusters with plump, unwrinkled berries	2-3 days
Lemons and Limes	thin-skinned and plump	1 month
Mango	firm and unblemished, fruity aroma	1 week
Cantaloupe Melon	blossom end should give with slight pressure	3-5 days
Oranges	thin skins, plump, unblemished	2-3 weeks
Peaches	creamy yellow background, unwrinkled skin	7-10 days
Pears	unblemished, yields to gentle pressure	1 week
Pineapple	reddish-gold, heavy, strong pineapple aroma	1-2 days
Plums	good color, yields to gentle pressure	3-5 days
Raspberries	plump, wine-red	1 day

CHOOSING

Fish and meats are the most expensive item on your shopping list so it's important to shop carefully. Fish should be displayed on ice. Look for clear eyes and firm flesh with no fishy odors. Likewise, meats should be bright red and odorless. The tougher cuts such as chuck are full of flavor but should be cooked by a moist method as in stews in casseroles. Tender cuts such as filet mignon and sirloin may be cooked quickly.

STORING

When you get home, rinse fish in cold water and pat dry with paper towels. Wrap tightly in plastic bag or plastic wrap, and store in the coldest party of the refrigerator (35°F to 40°F). For best flavor and texture, use as soon as possible after buying, preferably the same day.

Meat should be removed from its store wrappings as soon as you get home. Divide into family or single/double sized portions, whatever is appropriate. Pat dry with paper towels and wrap loosely in plastic wrap or parchment paper before refrigerating. The air circulation discourages the growth of bacteria.

Use these guidelines for optimal flavor and freshness of fish and meat.

FISH or MEAT	Refrigerator TIME	Freezer TIME
Bacon	5-7 days	3-4 weeks
Bluefish Fillets	1-2 days	2-3 months
Chops	3-4 days	4-6 months
Cooked Chicken	2-3 days	3-4 months
Cooked Ham Slices	3-4 days	1-2 months
Cooked Meats	3-4 days	2-3 months
Cooked/Breaded Fish	2-3 days	2-3 months
Cut Up Chicken	1-2 days	6-9 months
Flounder Fillets	1-2 days	4 months
Ground Beef	1-2 days	3-4 months
Halibut Steaks	1-2 days	2-3 months
Mackerel	1-2 days	2-3 months
Red Snapper Fillets	1-2 days	4 months
Roasts	2-3 days	8-12 months
Salmon Steaks and Fillets	1-2 days	2-3 months
Shrimp (Cooked)	2-3 days	1-2 months
Shrimp (Uncooked)	1-2 days	3-4 months
Steaks	2-3 days	8-12 months
Trout	1-2 days	2-3 months
Tuna Steaks	1-2 days	2-3 months
Whole Chicken	1-2 days	10-12 months
Whole/Half Fully Cooked Ham	5-7 days	1-2 months

TOOLS

*U*TENSILS & APPLIANCES

As cooks, we wouldn't be creating much of anything without the right tools—utensils and appliances—to work with. Here's sound advice on what you need, and what features are essential, to do the jobs right.

Cooking is creative and satisfying. But for ease as well as consistency and accuracy, it's important to have the right tools. Know the characteristics of each type of cookware and utensils so that you can use the right piece of equipment for the job. Knowing how to use these tools, and how they work, will go far in helping make you an even better cook.

Consider weight and shape. Get the feel by handling before buying. Hand-held utensils should be comfortable to hold and manipulate. Look for items that are easy to clean, with few grooves. You want pieces that come apart. Buy dishwasher safe and nonstick items when possible, noting that kitchen knives and wooden spoons should not go into the dishwasher. Don't skimp on price; usually the more expensive will last indefinitely.

Of course, the cheapest and often the most effective utensils are your clean-washed hands. They make the quickest work of everyday chores like shaping meat loaves and burgers, rubbing fats into dry ingredients such as streusel toppings, and so much more.

SMALL UTENSILS

Handheld items such as wooden spoons and whisks should be sturdy but comfortable to hold. All these items are inexpensive, so buy the best. Another idea: Double up on measuring cups and spoons; this avoids washing between wet and dry measurements in one recipe.

Colander: Choose a sturdy, metal colander with handles on each side. You'll need this for draining vegetables, pasta and other liquid and solid ingredients.

Graduated Measuring Spoons: Look for those that range from 1/8 teaspoon to 1 tablespoon. Available in metal or heavy plastic.

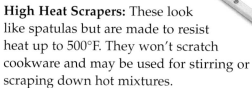

High Heat Scrapers: These look like spatulas but are made to resist heat up to 500°F. They won't scratch cookware and may be used for stirring or scraping down hot mixtures.

Ladle: Choose a long-handled metal ladle with a deep bowl. For transferring soups and stews from pot to plate or serving bowls.

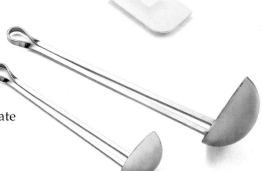

Measuring Cups: Look for glass or sturdy plastic with both U.S. and metric measurements. Avoid metal; it becomes hot when measuring hot liquids. Available in sizes from 1 to 8 cups, but a 4-cup model is most versatile. Read at eye level while the cup is on a flat surface. You also need a set of graduated nested measuring cups ranging from 1/4 cup to 1 cup for measuring dry ingredients, oils and shortening.

Mixing Bowls: Nests of bowls ranging from small to large are practical since they don't take up a lot of storage space. Available in glass, metal and durable plastic, the last may be fitted with a rubber ring on the bottom to avoid slippage. Useful for melting butter and chocolate, and cooking in the microwave.

Spatulas: Available in plastic, rubber or metal. Rubber is more flexible for baking tasks, but sturdy enough for scraping every bit of mixture from the mixing bowl and folding mixtures such as angel food cakes or omelets. Metal spatulas are wider, with slats for drainage; use them to turn solid foods as in frying or lifting foods from a pan to avoid breaking.

Mixing Spoons: Available in wooden or plastic; all-purpose for mixing and stirring. These should be sturdy and easy to hold. Buy at least one with an extra-long handle so that your hand doesn't get hot when stirring hot mixtures.

Timer: Look for an easy-to-read dial with a long ring alarm. Should monitor up to 1 hour cooking time.

Pastry Blender: If you're planning to make your own pastry on a regular basis, this is essential. Quickly and evenly cuts solid fats into flour.

Tongs: Buy all-metal tongs for turning deep-fried items and transferring foods from pan to serving dishes. Plastic-coated handles give a good grip.

Wire Whisk: Invest in two sizes. The smaller is essential to whisk small quantities such as salad dressing. The larger is essential for whisking batters, and avoiding or breaking down lumps in sauces and gravies.

Sieve: Most flours today are pre-sifted but you'll need this to sift dry ingredients for a particularly light sponge cake, and to separate solids and liquids from a mixture.

Slotted Spoons: For removing foods from boiling liquids, for testing pasta *al dente*, and to skim the froth off soups as they begin to boil.

KITCHEN GADGETS

There's an entire array of necessary gadgets that will make life in the kitchen much easier.

Apple Corer: This tool removes the apple's core and seeds cleanly so that apples may be stuffed for baking, cut into apple rings, or made into wedges for poaching. Made of metal with a sturdy handle, often of wood and comfortable to hold. Press firmly down through the center of the apple.

Can Opener: You may have an electric opener but it's a good idea to have a sturdy, hand-held opener as a back-up. Look for good cutting edges, a comfortable handle, and an attached bottle opener.

Candy, Jelly and Deep-Fry Thermometer: Dual-purpose with readings for candy and jelly making, and deep fat frying. Temperatures should register from 100°F to 400°F. Choose a thermometer with a heatproof handle and adjustable clip so that the thermometer can be attached to the pan.

Citrus Juice Squeezer: Glass or plastic. The bowl underneath the strainer catches the juice, while the seeds and pulp are retained in the strainer.

Citrus Zester: Use to shave off strips of citrus zest (the rind with no white and bitter pith attached.) The blade is made of metal but the handle may be of wood, plastic or other material. Choose a sturdy zester as you need to press hard.

Corkscrew: There is a huge variety of corkscrews available from the inexpensive giveaways to artful items. Choose one with good leverage and a hinged blade to help you remove foil.

Egg Separator: A shallow shaped cup with a narrow slit so that the egg white slips out and the yolk remains in the cup.

Garlic Press: Choose a heavy, metal press with sturdy handles. The grill should detach for easy cleaning.

Graters: There are two types, the box grater and flat grater (shown). Both have large and small holes. The box grater is nice to use as it stands firmly on a flat surface. Wash with a soft brush under running water immediately after use.

Instant Read Thermometer: For meats. Have a dial with a 5- to 8-inch probe to be inserted in the thickest part of the meat. Readings obtained in seconds.

Kitchen Scissors: An indispensable timesaving item. To cut and snip fresh herbs, dice cooked bacon, and trim leaves from vegetables and flowers.

Nutmeg Grater: A small grater with tiny holes used for grating nutmeg as needed. There's usually a small compartment in the top to store the whole nutmeg.

Oil Sprayer: Sprays oil evenly over vegetables, meats and poultry before being broiled or grilled. Cylindrical, usually made of metal with a plastic pump insert.

Pepper and Salt Mill: Fresh ground pepper has a pungency lacking in the packaged, ground product. Salt mills are used for grinding large sea salt crystals. Mills are of varying sizes and materials (such as glass or wood) and may be decorative.

Refrigerator and Freezer Thermometer: Hangs or stands with a dial, which may read from -20°F to 80°F.

Swivel Peeler: Use for peeling vegetables such as potatoes and carrots. Made of metal. Look for non-slip, easy-grip handles to absorb pressure while you work.

POTS

Your kitchen should contain at least 3 deep pots of high quality, and a steamer basket.

Dutch Oven: A large, squat pot with two handles. Big enough to hold a large bird or roast. Sizes range from 2 to 8 quarts.

Pressure Cooker: Cooks food faster at higher temperatures. A good pressure cooker is made of a highly conductive metal like aluminum or stainless steel with a copper, sandwiched base. Safety valves and automatic lid locks are always included. Carefully follow manufacturer's directions.

Stock Pot: A tall, wide pot with straight sides, from a smaller version which holds 6 to 8 quarts to a large model holding 16 to 20 quarts. Essential for making stock and large quantities of soups.

Steamer Basket: A metal, colander-like basket which stands on short legs inside a pan partially filled with boiling water. Used for steaming fish and vegetables. Collapsible for easy storage.

PANS

Pans are some of the most expensive items in your kitchen. They will be used constantly, so buy the very best you can afford—they can last a lifetime. Sets are a good buy but only if you use all the pieces. It may be cheaper to buy the individual pieces you constantly use. Materials vary and include cast iron, stainless steel, aluminum and copper.

Double Boiler: Basically two saucepans in one. A smaller pan is placed inside a larger one that is partially filled with water. The food (usually a sauce) is gently cooked over simmering water so there's no danger of scorching or curdling.

Frying Pan or Skillet: Usually 1 to $2^1/2$ inches deep, with gently sloping sides for easy turning and removal of food. Choose one with a long, heatproof handle. Sizes range from small (7- or 8-inch diameter), medium (9- or 10-inch diameter) and large (11- or 12-inch diameter).

Omelet Pan: Best to buy a nonstick model. Approximately 6-inch size for a 2-egg omelet but they also come in 7- and 9-inch sizes.

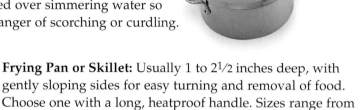

Roaster: Shallow pan large enough to hold roasts and big birds. Should include a rack and lid.

Saucepan: Usually straight or slightly sloping high sides of 4 to 7 inches high, with a long handle. Range in sizes from about 1 pint to 4 quarts. All-purpose from making sauces to heating foods.

Stove-Top Grilling Pan: For a char-grilled look. Choose a flat pan with deep ridges and a removable handle for easy storage.

Wok: An all-purpose Asian cooking pan with high sloping sides. Resembles a bowl. The traditional wok is 14 inches in diameter and made of carbon steel. Used for stir-fries and Asian cooking.

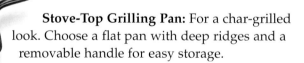

BAKING NECESSITIES

Baking is a breeze with these indispensable basics. Buy nonstick when available. Most items are dishwasher safe, but check and follow manufacturer's directions.

Baking Dishes: Approximately 2 inches deep, baking dishes may be ceramic or of a heatproof substance such as Pyrex or Corningware. Available in various sizes, 8- or 9-inch squares are most useful, as is the 15x10x1-inch size. Use for cakes, lasagna or casseroles.

Cookie Cutters: These come in all shapes and sizes. The most useful are nests of fluted and plain cutters. Choose metal, which makes cutting through dough easier; never buy plastic.

Cookie Sheets: Choose shiny, nonstick sheets, preferably open on three sides so cookies brown evenly. Insulated cookie sheets are available —a bit pricier but worth it as they prevent cookies from becoming too dark on the bottom.

Flour Sifter: Sprinkles flour evenly over a pastry board before rolling out pastry. Also sifts confectioner's sugar over cakes and cookies.

Layer Cake Pan: A loose bottomed pan about 8-inches in diameter. For layer cakes, nonstick is preferable.

Loaf Pans: Come in varying sizes including mini-loaf size. Nonstick is best. Use for breads, coffeecakes and pâtés.

Muffin Tins: In trays of 12 regular or 12 miniature size muffins. Buy nonstick, but always spray with nonstick vegetable spray. Use for muffins or Yorkshire pudding, an accompaniment to roast beef.

Narrow Spatulas: These have a long, narrow, flexible blade. Use for spreading frostings and fillings, and to loosen cakes from baking pans. Not for cutting.

Oven Thermometer: The most common is  one with a dial that hangs or stands on the oven shelf and measures from 200°F to 550°F. Check oven temperatures periodically. Unless you have your oven recalibrated annually, chances are that the actual temperature will differ from the oven settings you choose.

Pastry Brush: Look for natural bristles and a wooden handle. For sealing, brushing egg wash on baked goods and melted butter on filo leaves. Do not place pastry brushes in the dishwasher.

Pie Pans: These have sloping sides and a lip for pie edging. Pie pans may be  made of metal, ovenproof glass or ceramic. Glass makes it easy to see how quickly the pie is cooking and browning on the bottom.

Pie Weights: Used for "baking blind" or weighing down a pastry shell during baking so that it does not rise. Available in ceramic and metal, weights should be completely cooled before returning to the container. Dried beans may also be used but are lighter and eventually need to be discarded.

Rolling Pin: Essential for pastry making. Choose one that is heavy, made of wood and without handles. This makes it easier to roll pastry out evenly.

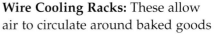

Sheet Cake Pans: May measure approximately 13x9 inches to 11x9 inches with deep sides. If nonstick, remove baked goods carefully to avoid scratching the pan's coating.

Springform Pan: A round cake pan with a clasp on the side, which opens to release the bottom. Springform pans may come in sets of three varying sizes. They must be lined and well-greased even if nonstick. Use for cheesecakes and tortes.

Wire Cooling Racks: These allow air to circulate around baked goods so that they cool faster. Racks come in several sizes.

KNIVES

You can't cook without good, sharp knives. The best are made of high-carbon stainless steel and are either forged from molded and hammered steel, or stamped (cut from a metal sheet). Invest in a wooden block for storage. If kept in a drawer where they can rattle around, knives will quickly lose their sharpness.

Carving Knife: An 8-inch, thin flexible blade used for slicing cooked meats, such as turkeys or roasts, to any thickness desired.

Bread Knife: Has a serrated 8$1/2$-inch blade used for slicing and cutting bread. This knife should not be sharpened.

Chef's Knife: Also known as a cook's knife or French knife. An all-purpose knife with an 8-inch blade. If you can only start out with one good knife, this is it.

Paring Knife: A small knife with 4-inch blade for paring or peeling fruits and vegetables.

Sharpening Steel: The essential tool for keeping the edge of your knives in prime condition. It does not sharpen. Rather, a sharpening steel is used in between sharpenings to extend the life of the edge. When the knife doesn't feel sharp any more after "steeling", bring it to a professional sharpener.

Boning Knife: Used for removing meat from the bone of cooked or uncooked poultry or beef. Unless you plan to bone your poultry, you may not need this knife.

Fillet Knife: Flexible and razor-sharp, this is a necessity for deboning your fresh catch.

Utility Knife: This fills the gap between the chef's knife and a paring knife. Cuts and pares vegetables and sandwiches.

SMALL ELECTRICS

In most contemporary kitchens, storage space is at a premium. Here are the essential small appliances.

Blender: Use to quickly chop or puree liquid mixtures such as soups, drinks and batters. Should have a heavy motor and glass or heavy plastic jar with a tight-fitting lid. Two or three speeds are sufficient.

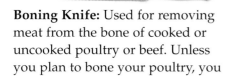

Electric Tea Kettle: Automatically shuts off when water is boiling. Look for one with a retractable cord.

Food processor: Quickly mixes and blends ingredients and chops fruits and herbs in seconds. Mini-processors are also available to chop small quantities of fresh herbs. Look for a model with a large plastic bowl, with blades and attachments for chopping, slicing, grating and mixing.

Bread Machine: Will mix, knead, rinse and bake the loaf. Machines range in size and shape as will loaves.

Electric Knife: Saves time and mess. Look for one with any easy-to-grip handle.

Hand-Held Mixer: Eliminates the need for a free-standing electric mixer, saving you valuable counter space. Choose one with three speeds and easily removable beaters.

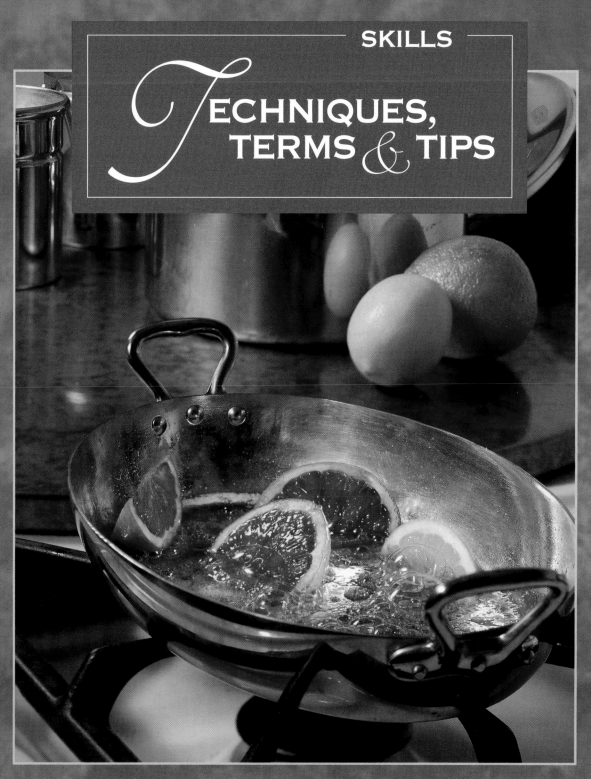

TECHNIQUES, TERMS & TIPS

Fresh ingredients and the proper tools start you on the road to cooking success. But what you do with these components—the skills and knowledge you apply—makes all the difference. These cooking techniques, definitions and tips will guide you to more cooking success.

SKILLS: Techniques, TERMS & TIPS

DRY HEAT COOKING METHODS

▲ **Bake and Roast:** To cook in an uncovered pan in an oven. This would apply to cakes and cookies, pies, vegetables, poultry, and cuts of beef.

▲ **Barbecue:** To grill over hot coals or on a gas or electric grill. Food is often basted with a spicy sauce while cooking.

Deep Fat Frying: Where food is totally immersed in hot vegetable oils in a deep, heavy pot. Ideally, food should be lowered into the hot fat in a wire basket so that it may be removed safely and easily. This also allows for a lot of the fat to drain off. Don't use butter or margarine; they have low smoking points so are not suitable.

Fat temperature is important. If fat isn't hot enough, the food will absorb the fat and make it soggy; measure temperature with a thermometer (350°F to 375°F is suitable for most frying). Or test with a 1-inch piece of bread. If the bread turns brown in 60 seconds, the oil is ready to cook whatever you are adding.

▲ **Fry:** To cook in hot fat in a skillet over direct heat. Great for eggs, meat, fish and vegetables.

▲ Grill or Broil: To expose foods to strong, direct heat as in an oven broiler or on a charcoal or gas grill, and cooked to desired doneness, one side at a time.

Pan-broil: To cook in a hot, lightly greased skillet on the stove top. Good technique for thin, lean meats and fish.

▲ Stir-fry: A basic Chinese cooking method where thinly sliced foods are fried in a small amount of oil. Foods are stirred and tossed constantly until cooked.

Sauté: To cook in a small amount of fat in a skillet on the stove top over medium high heat. For best browning and flavor, use a combination of butter and oil. The butter gives flavor and the oil browns without burning.

MOIST HEAT COOKING METHODS

▲ Boil: To heat liquid to approximately 212°F over high heat until large bubbles surface and break. A rolling boil is when bubbles surface and break quickly. Parboiling is cooking briefly so food is partially cooked.

▲ Blanch: To plunge food (usually vegetables) briefly into boiling water to set the color, slightly tenderize and preserve nutrients, or to remove the skin as with tomatoes. Blanching also inactivates enzymes before freezing.

Braise: To cook slowly in a small amount of liquid in a tightly covered pot as in pot roasts and stews.

Crisp-Tender: To cook vegetables only until they are tenderized but still crisp and crunchy.

▲ Poach: To cook in a simmering liquid on the stove top over low heat, as in poultry and fish.

Simmer: To cook very gently, just below boiling point, on the stove top over very low heat. Simmering tenderizes tough foods, as in a stew, and protects delicate foods such as fish.

▲ Steam: To cook food over boiling water, using a steamer basket within a covered pan. A good method which helps retain maximum nutrition, color, texture and flavors.

Stew: Cooking long and slow in a covered pan in a small amount of liquid as in beef stews.

COOKING TERMS DEMYSTIFIED

How many of us really know the meaning of all the various cooking terms we hear and read? This outline should help you understand our wonderful pastime even more. Plus, it will serve as a handy reference.

Bain-Marie: A hot water bath that keeps cooked food hot. The container with food is set into a larger container containing hot water.

Baste: To spoon liquids over foods during cooking, as in roast chicken and turkey. Helps keep the food (often meat) moist and flavorful.

Batter: An uncooked mixture of a flour and liquid base. Batter may be as thin as unwhipped heavy cream, thin enough to pour as for pancakes, or thicker to spoon as for muffins.

Beat: To stir or mix ingredients rapidly until smooth, light and fluffy. Beating tools include a wire whisk or electric hand mixer.

Blend: To mix ingredients well using an electric blender or food processor.

Caramelize: To melt sugar over low heat until it becomes a golden brown syrup. Remove from the heat immediately and use as directed. To caramelize may also mean sprinkling sugar on top of a food such as a crème brûlée, then placing it under the broiler until melted and golden.

Chop: To cut into small, chunky pieces about the size of a small pea. "Finely chop" means even smaller pieces. Use a knife for small quantities, or the food processor fitted with a steel blade for larger quantities.

Core: To remove the center which contains the seeds of a hard fruit such as apples and pears. An apple corer makes this a one-step, easy process.

Correct the Seasoning: Taste first, then add seasonings included in the recipe to your personal taste.

Cube: To cut food into 1/2-inch squares or as directed in recipe using a knife.

Curdle: When a mixture separates into small clots. This may happen when beating eggs into a butter mixture. Avoid curdling by adding a tablespoon of flour to the eggs before beating.

Deglaze: After cooking meat or fish, browned bits may be stuck at the bottom of the pan. A small amount of liquid, usually stock or wine, is added and stirred with a wooden spoon to loosen. This process is called deglazing. The resulting flavorful liquid may be used as a sauce or sauce base.

Dice: To cut food into cubes about 1/4-inch using a knife.

Dissolve: When a dry ingredient is stirred into a liquid until the dry ingredient has completely disappeared. For example, flavored gelatin stirred into boiling water or sugar stirred into tea or coffee.

Dot: To scatter tiny bits of an ingredient, such as butter or margarine, over a dish, usually before cooking.

Dough: A mixture of flour, liquids and other ingredients stiff enough to be shaped, kneaded or rolled with a rolling pin as with pastry.

Drain: To separate liquids from solids. Use a colander or sieve.

Dredge: To toss foods in a dry mixture to coat lightly. One example: Chicken cutlets in breadcrumbs. Usually the food has been dipped in egg or milk before dredging, so that the dry mixture sticks to the food's surface.

Drizzle: To pour a liquid in a thin, uneven stream over food. Pour from the tip of a large spoon, or from a measuring cup.

Dust: To sprinkle lightly with a dry ingredient such as confectioner's sugar. A sieve gives a nice even finish.

Egg Separator: Separates egg whites from yolks.

Fillet: A boneless cut of meat, poultry or fish. Filleting means to remove the bones from meat or fish to make a fillet. (See p. 86)

Flake: To separate foods, usually cooked fish, following the natural slices. A fork makes this task easy.

Flute: To use your thumb and forefinger to make a decorative edge on pastry. Fluting can also mean making indentations on vegetables, such as radish roses using a sharp paring knife.

Flambé: Pouring warm liquor such as brandy over food, and lighting. A spectacular tableside serving method, as in bananas flambé.

Floret: Small clusters from a tight-budded vegetable such as cauliflower and broccoli.

COOKING TERMS CONTINUED

Fold: To use a rubber spatula to combine ingredients by cutting through a mixture vertically, then sliding across the bottom of the bowl and around the sides so that the mixture turns over. For combining heavy mixtures into lighter ones.

Glaze: Coating a food with a warm sauce, jam or other ingredients to give a glossy finish.

Grate: To rub foods on the holes of a grater for thin shreds or particles.

Grease: To rub the cooking surface of a pan or cooking utensil with melted shortening using a pastry brush. This prevents foods from sticking. Nonstick cooking spray may also be used.

Hulling: To remove the green caps from stem ends of fruits such as strawberries.

Julienne: To cut in thin, match-like sticks, about 1/8-inch thick and 2-inches long. Use a paring knife. for small items such as carrots. Use a larger knife for large items such as rutabagas.

Knead: To work a stiff flour-based mixture, such as bread dough, on a floured surface. Use the heel of your hand for a fold-and-press process for 10 to 15 minutes or until the dough is smooth and satiny and does not stick to the board. (See p. 61)

Lukewarm: Approximately 95°F. Alternatively, when sprinkled on the inside of the wrist, liquids should feel neither hot or cold.

Marinade: A seasoned, acidic based (with wine or vinegar) liquid mixture used to help tenderize and flavor meats.

Marinate: To soak a food in a marinade using a glass or non-metal dish. Marinate in the refrigerator.

Mash: To press vegetables (usually potatoes) with a potato masher or large fork to a coarse or fairly smooth pulp.

Mince: To chop food very finely. Mincing may be done in the food processor.

Peak Softly: Egg whites beaten with electric mixer just until the peaks droop downwards. Stiff peaks occur when the beaten egg whites stand up straight without drooping.

Pinch: The amount of a dry ingredient which can be held between your thumb and forefinger. Less than 1/8 teaspoon.

Reduce: Cooking a liquid, uncovered, to decrease the quantity of liquid and increase flavor. The liquid will thicken slightly as it is reduced.

Roux: A mixture of fat and flour, cooked over medium-low heat, so that the starch granules are cooked and the raw floury taste disappears. A cooked roux can vary in color from off-white to light brown, depending on the recipe. A roux is used to thicken stock or sauce.

Scald: To heat a liquid, usually milk, until tiny bubbles form at the sides of the pan, just before boiling.

Score: To use a sharp knife to make shallow cuts, about 1/8 to 1/4 inch thick, across the surface of foods before cooking. Gives an attractive appearance to hams and breads.

Sear: To brown the surfaces of a food, usually meat, over high heat in order to seal in the juices. In stews, this helps meats retain flavor.

Shred: To cut foods into long, thin strips using a sharp knife or the shredding blade on a food processor. Cabbage and hard cheeses are often shredded.

Skim: To remove the foam (scum) or fat from the surface of liquids using a large metal spoon or bulb baster.

Slice: To cut flat pieces to a desired thickness.

Smoke Point: The temperature where heated fat begins to smoke and give off harsh, burning smells.

Snip: To cut into small pieces with kitchen scissors. Snipping is indispensable for the best taste of fresh herbs. This technique also eliminates the need to clean a chopping board and knives.

Tent: A loose covering of aluminum foil to prevent excess browning of roasts and oven-cooked foods.

Toss: To gently lift and mix ingredients, such as in vegetables and salads.

Zest: The thin outer peel of citrus fruits without any of the bitter white pith.

SAFE COOKING

Here are some important guidelines to follow to assure that your food and cooking techniques combine for a healthful and wholesome end product.

- Wash hands with soap and water for at least 20 seconds before and after handling foods. Cross-contamination is especially high when handling raw meats and seafood. Keep these foods away from ready-to-eat foods.

- Wash cutting boards, dishes, utensils and counter tops with hot soapy water after preparing each food item and before you go on to the next. You can use antibacterial spray too (shown), but rinse well before letting food come in contact again.

- Use hard plastic or other non-porous cutting boards for cutting raw meats. After use, run cutting boards through the dishwasher after removing any food particles, or thoroughly wash with hot soapy water and a brush, then rinse with cold water. Do not use wood cutting boards! They trap bacteria in the grooves made by your knife.

- If you use cloth towels rather than paper towels, wash often with a little bleach, in the hottest cycle your washing machine offers.

- Always wash fruits and vegetables before eating and cooking.

EASY COOKING

There's no need to make cooking a chore. It should always be fun. These ideas should help you in that pursuit.

- Read the recipe through. Make sure all ingredients are on hand and placed on your counter along with utensils needed.

- Defrost frozen foods in the refrigerator or under cold running water, not at room temperature.

- Before scalding milk, rinse a pan with cold water. This helps avoid scorching.

- Use kitchen scissors to snip fresh herbs.

- Keep an oil sprayer on hand to spray baking dishes and vegetables to be grilled, or use non-stick vegetable spray.

- When thawing foods, protect your refrigerator and its contents from uncooked toxins. A plate works well.

- Never place cooked food on a plate that previously held raw meats or seafood.

- Cover leftovers tightly before reheating thoroughly. Liquids such as gravies should be brought to a rolling boil.

- Never leave food that should be refrigerated out for more than two hours, only one hour if outdoors and the temperature is above 90°F.

- Marinate raw meats, fish and poultry in a glass dish in the refrigerator, not at room temperature. If you want to use some of the marinade as a dip or basting sauce, set some aside before adding the raw foods.

- Cook meat and poultry completely at one time. Partial cooking may encourage bacterial growth. Use a meat thermometer to gauge accurate doneness.

- In most recipes, you can reduce calories by using reduced-fat or skim dairy products.

- Reduce cholesterol by substituting 2 egg whites for 1 whole egg.

- Freeze any bones, meats and vegetables for making stock at a later date.

- Abandon guilt! Many convenience foods are top quality and as good as homemade. For speedy cooking: use prepared puff pastry and pie shells for pastries and pies; substitute canned broth or bouillon cubes for stock; use frozen or refrigerated minced garlic instead of fresh; and exchange frozen or canned fruits and vegetables for fresh produce.

HEALTHY EATING

Cookbooks focus on the "how" of cooking—the fun stuff —and not the "what" and "how much" of eating— factors with real effect on your health and well-being. Here are some guidelines in that respect.

WHAT'S A SERVING?

Probably not what you're used to! In the United States, portion sizes are way out of control. According to restaurants and fast food eateries, bigger is better. But for healthy, daily eating, moderation is the key. Get to know what reasonably sized portions are.

SOME HEALTHY DINING IDEAS

Here are a few great ideas for eating healthier and feeling better. They work!

- Put less food on your plate or use a smaller plate. At restaurants, eat a reasonable portion and take the rest home for another meal. Or an obliging waiter may serve half and pack half.

- Share a meal. When eating out, consider sharing an appetizer or splitting an entrée with a friend. Even if there's a small charge for sharing, it's worth it.

- Slow down: It takes about 20 minutes to feel full. Eat slowly, chew well and taste the food. Put down your knife and fork between mouthfuls. You'll leave the table feeling satisfied after a reasonable portion, instead of bloated from overeating.

WHAT DOES A PORTION LOOK LIKE?
REASONABLY-SIZED PORTIONS

Grains	1 sandwich slice,
	1/2 cup bread
	1 cup ready-to-eat cooked cereal, rice or pasta
	1/2 small bagel
Vegetables	1 cup cooked (about the size of a baseball)
	3/4 cup vegetable juice
Fruits	1 medium apple, banana, orange or pear
	1/2 cup cooked or canned fruit juice
	3/4 cup 100% fruit juice
Milk, yogurt, cheese	1 cup milk or yogurt
	1 1/2 oz. unprocessed cheese
Meat, poultry, fish, dried beans, eggs and nuts	3 to 4 oz. cooked lean meat, poultry or fish
	1 cup cooked beans
	1 egg
	2 tablespoons peanut butter
	1/3 cup nuts

NUTRITION FACTS

THE FOOD GUIDE PYRAMID

The Food Guide Pyramid is an educational guide from the U.S. Department of Agriculture and U.S. Department of Health and Human Services. Use it as a guide to the recommended number of daily servings from each food group for a balanced and healthy diet.

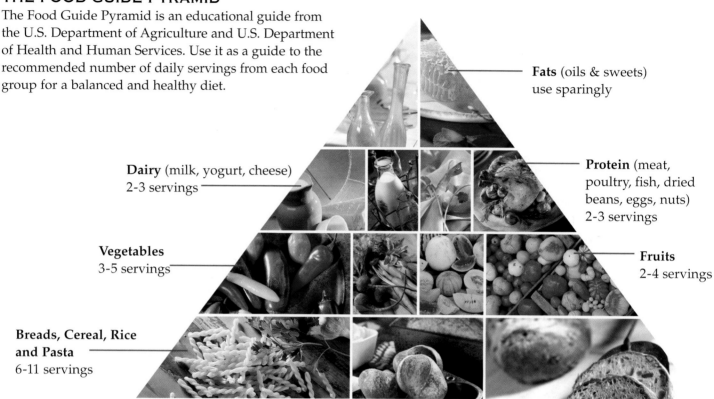

Fats (oils & sweets) use sparingly

Dairy (milk, yogurt, cheese) 2-3 servings

Protein (meat, poultry, fish, dried beans, eggs, nuts) 2-3 servings

Vegetables 3-5 servings

Fruits 2-4 servings

Breads, Cereal, Rice and Pasta 6-11 servings

NUTRITION TERMS

Calorie: A unit used to measure energy, specifically heat, needed to raise the temperature of 1 gram of water 1°C. All calories are equal no matter from what source. Fat contains more calories per gram than either protein and carbohydrate.

> 1 gram fat = 9 calories
>
> 1 gram protein = 4 calories
>
> 1 gram carbohydrate = 4 calories

Fat: Provides essential nutrients to the body, is needed for healthy skin. It also cushions vital organs and acts as insulation from cold.

Cholesterol: Is a fatty like substance produced by our bodies, which we cannot do without. Too much may result in a plaque build-up in the arteries—the reason for the close watch kept on cholesterol.

Dietary Fiber: Plant foods that are not broken down or absorbed. A complex carbohydrate.

Protein: Daily infusions of top-quality proteins are needed to sustain life. Complete proteins such as dairy products, meat and fish contain all the amino acids needed; incomplete proteins, such as legumes, lack some essential amino acids and should be supplemented with another food that supplies the missing acid.

Carbohydrates: Sugars and starches providing the body with fuel and energy. Athletes stoke up on complex carbohydrates such as pasta and grains before a game.

APPETIZERS & SNACKS

Expand your repertoire of appetizers and snacks! Here are the essential recipes you'll need sooner or later, and a selection of superb master recipes to use when you want to create even more taste and variety.

ESSENTIAL

CHEESE FONDUE – BASEL STYLE

For a fun supper, serve this fondue with a crisp green salad and chilled white wine.

3	cups (12 oz.) shredded Swiss cheese
3	cups (12 oz.) shredded Gruyère cheese
2	cups (8 oz.) shredded Emmentaler cheese
2	tablespoons cornstarch
1	garlic clove, halved
4	cups dry white wine
2 to 3	tablespoons kirsch
	Dash nutmeg
2	loaves French bread, cut into 2-inch chunks

1. In large bowl, combine cheeses and cornstarch; set aside.

2. Rub inside of large pot with garlic; leave garlic in pot. Pour in wine; heat over medium heat until tiny bubbles begin to form at edges. Reduce heat to very low.

3. Add cheese mixture by handfuls, stirring constantly with wooden spoon. Continue stirring 10 to 15 minutes or until cheese is melted. Stir in kirsch and nutmeg.

4. Transfer cheese mixture to fondue warmer; set in center of table along with bowl of bread chunks. Spear chunks and swirl in hot fondue.

6 to 8 servings.

Preparation time: 30 minutes.
Ready to serve: 1 hour.

Per serving: 930 calories, 45.5 g fat (28 g saturated fat), 140 mg cholesterol, 1070 mg sodium, 3.5 g fiber.

The best fondue is made with a mixture of cheeses. If you can't find Emmentaler, substitute Swiss or Gruyère from Switzerland. Bread should be cut the day before and stand, uncovered, at room temperature to firm up. This prevents chunks breaking off into the fondue while dunking. Kirsch, available in small bottles from your liquor store, is a clear and potent brandy distilled from cherries.

DEVILED EGGS

The smooth, fluffy filling is lightened and expanded by blending in part-skim ricotta cheese. You'll find there's plenty of mixture to pile high into each egg white cavity.

6 hard-cooked eggs, shelled
1/3 cup part-skim ricotta cheese
1/4 cup reduced-fat mayonnaise
1 tablespoon butter, softened
1 teaspoon white vinegar
1/4 teaspoon salt
3 drops hot pepper sauce
1/8 teaspoon paprika

1 Cut eggs in half lengthwise. Remove yolks and place in food processor. Cut a thin slice from the bottom of each egg so it stands securely on the serving dish without tipping. Add slices to yolks.

2 Add cheese, mayonnaise, butter, vinegar, salt and hot pepper sauce to food processor; process until mixture is smooth.

3 Spoon rounded tablespoonfuls of mixture into each egg cavity, or pipe mixture into eggs with large star tip. Cover with plastic wrap and chill. Remove from refrigerator 30 minutes before serving. Dust with paprika.

12 servings.

Preparation time: 30 minutes.
Ready to serve: 1 hour, 30 minutes.

Per serving: 70 calories, 5.5 g fat (2 g saturated fat), 110 mg cholesterol, 135 mg sodium, 0 g fiber.

VARIATION **Herb-Spiked Deviled Eggs**
Add 2 tablespoons finely chopped fresh parsley or chives to filling; garnish with parsley sprig or tiny spears of chive.

VARIATION **Tuna-Filled Deviled Eggs**
Combine egg yolks with 1/2 cup tuna, 2 tablespoons mustard and 1 tablespoon lemon juice. Season with salt and pepper. Process until smooth. Garnish with lemon peel.

To make hard-cooked eggs without a green ring around the yolk, cover eggs with cold water to about 1 inch above the eggs. Bring to a boil, cover and turn off heat. Let eggs stand in the hot water 15 minutes for large eggs, a minute or two less for medium eggs. Pour off hot water. Cover with cold water to which 1 or 2 cups of ice cubes have been added. Let cool. Remove shell by cracking gently against side of pan. Shells will come off easily under cold running water.

STUFFED CELERY STICKS

If desired, an additional 1/2 cup whipped cream cheese may be substituted for the goat cheese. Belgian endive leaves also make an attractive veggie container in lieu of celery.

1	cup (4 oz.) goat cheese
1/4	cup cream cheese, whipped
2	tablespoons sour cream
2	teaspoons finely chopped chives
1/8	lemon-pepper seasoning
12	ribs celery, cut into 3 1/2-inch pieces
3	dozen small ripe olives, pitted
10 to 15	chives cut into 1-inch lengths

1. In medium bowl, beat goat cheese, cream cheese, sour cream and chopped chives at medium speed until smooth. Season with lemon pepper.

2. Spoon enough mixture onto each celery rib to cover about one-third of length. Garnish with 1 olive and 2 or 3 chive "spears" at end of each celery rib.

30 to 36 sticks.

Preparation time: 30 minutes.
Ready to serve: 30 minutes.

Per serving: 25 calories, 2 g fat (1 g saturated fat), 5 mg cholesterol, 75 mg sodium, 0.5 g fiber.

SIMA'S GRAVLAX

I had no idea that Gravlax, a Scandinavian specialty, was so easy to make until I got this recipe from my friend Sima Radovitz. The thinly sliced, cured salmon is very expensive to purchase, but the price is slashed when you prepare Gravlax at home with this recipe.

1	(1 1/2-lb.) boneless salmon fillet
3/4	cup kosher (coarse) salt
1/4	cup granulated sugar
1	large bunch dill

1. Rinse salmon and pat dry. Set aside.

2. In small bowl, combine salt and sugar; mix well. Spread one-half of the dill in 3-quart casserole; sprinkle with one-half of the salt mixture.

3. Place salmon, skin side down, in casserole. Cover with remaining dill and salt mixtures, pressing mixtures into surface of salmon. Wrap fish tightly with parchment paper, then plastic wrap.

4. Weigh down casserole with 5-lb. weight (I use a 5-lb. bag of sugar or flour wrapped in a plastic bag.) Refrigerate 2 days, turning once.

5. Unwrap fish; run under cold water to remove dill and salt mixtures. If too salty, soak in cold water 30 minutes; pat dry.

6. With sharp knife, slice salmon paper thin on the diagonal. Serve with sliced pumpernickel, bagels and cream cheese.

10 to 15 servings.

Preparation time: 30 minutes.
Ready to serve: 2 days.

Per serving: 100 calories, 4 g total fat (1 g saturated fat), 45 mg cholesterol, 1380 g sodium, 0 g fiber.

Gravlax may be refrigerated 3 to 4 days. If wrapped tightly, it may be frozen. Remove from freezer to refrigerator 24 hours before needed.

SIMA'S GRAVLAX

FRESH HERB PESTO

Any mixture of green herbs may be used for this pesto. Freeze the mixture in an ice cube tray. Store the frozen cubes in the freezer, in a small plastic bag, and use them as needed.

>   2   garlic cloves, halved
>   1/3 cup walnuts
>   2   cups loosely-packed fresh basil
>   2   cups loosely-packed fresh parsley sprigs
>   1/3 cup olive oil
>   1/4 cup (1 oz.) freshly grated Parmesan cheese
>   1/8 teaspoon salt
>   1/8 teaspoon freshly ground pepper

① In food processor, coarsely chop garlic and walnuts. Add basil and parsley; finely chop. With motor running, pour in olive oil and Parmesan cheese; process to blend. Season with salt and pepper.

About 1 cup.

Preparation time: 5 minutes.
Ready to serve: 10 minutes.

Per serving: 80 calories, 1 g fat (0 g saturated fat), 0 mg cholesterol, 50 mg sodium, 2 g fiber.

MEXICAN COPANATA

Don't let this rather long list of ingredients scare you. All the chopping is done in the food processor, and if you like, 1 cup of frozen chopped onions may be substituted for 1 medium onion. Serve this zesty dip with warm pita bread triangles.

>   1   medium onion, cut into 1-inch pieces
>   4   plum tomatoes, cut into 1-inch pieces
>   4   tomatillos, cut into 1-inch pieces
>   1/4 cup chopped fresh cilantro
>   3   tablespoons olive oil
>   1   eggplant, cut into 1-inch pieces
>   1/2 cup oil-cured ripe olives, pitted
>   1/2 cup tomato sauce
>   1/4 cup tomato paste
>   3   tablespoons pine nuts
>   3   tablespoons dried currants
>   1   tablespoon cumin
>   1/2 teaspoon crushed red pepper
>   1/8 teaspoon salt

① In food processor, coarsely chop onion, tomatoes and tomatillos. Add cilantro; process an additional 2 minutes. Set aside.

② In large skillet, heat olive oil over medium-high heat until hot. Sauté eggplant 2 to 3 minutes or until just brown at edges.

③ Reduce heat to low; add chopped tomato mixture, olives, tomato sauce, tomato paste, pine nuts, currants, cumin and red pepper. Stir to mix well.

④ Cook slowly, stirring often, 20 to 30 minutes or until mixture has thickened. Serve at room temperature.

3 1/2 to 4 cups.

Preparation time: 25 minutes.
Ready to serve: 1 hour.

Per serving: 70 calories, 4 g fat (0.5 g saturated fat), 0 mg cholesterol, 160 mg sodium, 2.5 g fiber.

Tomatillos are a popular ingredient in Mexican and Southwestern cuisine. They resemble little green tomatoes, but are covered with a papery husk that must be removed before use. Tomatillos add a unique fruity flavor to vegetable dips, salads and chilled soups.

MEXICAN COPANATA

PESTO-STUFFED MUSHROOMS

Red cherry tomatoes add a nice texture contrast and a splash of bright color. These mushrooms may be assembled and refrigerated, then cooked before serving. Double the recipe to make a pretty platter on a cocktail buffet or create a dinner party side dish.

12	medium mushrooms
1/4	cup *Fresh Herb Pesto* (page 50)
1/2	cup fresh bread crumbs
4	tablespoons olive oil
6	red grape or cherry tomatoes

① Heat broiler. Spray broiler pan with nonstick cooking spray.

② Remove stems from mushrooms; cut stems into small pieces. Place stems in food processor with Fresh Herb Pesto, bread crumbs and 1 tablespoon of the olive oil. Process 8 to 10 seconds or until mixture is combined and smooth.

③ Arrange mushroom caps frilly side up on broiler pan. Spray or brush with 1 tablespoon olive oil.

④ Divide pesto mixture evenly among mushroom caps.

⑤ Cut tomatoes in half lengthwise. Top each stuffed mushroom with one tomato half, cut side down. Spray or brush with remaining olive oil.

⑥ Place under broiler 3 to 5 minutes or until stuffing is just brown. Turn off broiler. Let mushrooms stand in oven an additional 5 minutes. Serve hot or at room temperature.

12 mushrooms.

Preparation time: 10 minutes.
Ready to serve: 20 minutes.

Per serving: 75 calories, 6 g fat (1 g saturated fat), 0 mg cholesterol, 55 mg sodium, 0.5 g fiber.

CHUTNEY BARBECUED CHICKEN WINGS

Instead of cooking on the barbecue, the wings may be arranged on a broiler pan and cooked under a preheated broiler, turning once. Save or freeze trimmed joints to add to a chicken stock.

2	lb. chicken wings
3/4	cup tomato chutney
3	tablespoons maple syrup
2	tablespoons fresh lemon juice
1	tablespoon low-sodium soy sauce
1 1/2	teaspoons minced garlic

① Cut off small third joint of each wing and discard or save for making stock. Separate first and second joints. Wash wings and pat dry. Arrange in single layer in 1 1/2-quart casserole.

② In small bowl, mix chutney with maple syrup, lemon juice, soy sauce and garlic. Pour over chicken wings, turning to coat evenly. Marinate 30 minutes in refrigerator.

③ Place chicken on gas grill over medium-high heat or on charcoal grill 4 to 6 inches from medium-high coals. Cook 5 to 7 minutes on each side or until internal temperature reaches at least 160°F.

16 to 20 wings.

Preparation time: 45 minutes.
Ready to serve: 1 hour.

Per serving: 60 calories, 4 g fat (1 g saturated fat), 15 mg cholesterol, 35 mg sodium, 0 g fiber.

THREE-PEPPER FRITTATA

A frittata is a vegetable omelet finished off by baking in the oven. Seasoned croutons are folded into this Italian-influenced dish so that it may double as a hearty snack or even a luncheon or supper dish. For cocktails, cut into small squares and insert a cocktail pick into each.

1/4 cup olive oil
1 large onion, chopped
1 large yellow bell pepper, seeded, diced
1 large orange bell pepper, seeded, diced
1 large red bell pepper, seeded, diced
8 eggs
1/2 cup chopped parsley
1 teaspoon lemon-pepper seasoning
1 1/2 cups seasoned croutons
3 tablespoons freshly grated Parmesan cheese

1. Heat broiler.
2. In large ovenproof skillet, heat olive oil over medium-high heat until hot. Sauté onions and bell peppers 5 minutes or until onions are tender.
3. In large bowl, whisk together eggs, parsley and lemon-pepper seasoning. Fold in croutons. Pour over vegetable mixture; reduce heat to low. Cook 10 to 15 minutes or until bottom is firm and golden brown. Sprinkle with cheese.
4. Place skillet under broiler. Cook 3 to 4 minutes or until egg mixture is set and top is just brown.
5. Let cool in skillet 5 minutes. Loosen sides with round-bladed knife before turning out onto platter. Cool to room temperature before cutting into squares.

About 4 dozen.

Preparation time: 20 minutes.
Ready to serve: 1 hour.

Per serving: 30 calories, 2 g fat (0.5 g saturated fat), 35 mg cholesterol, 30 mg sodium, 0.5 g fiber.

If the skillet handle is not ovenproof, wrap tightly with heavy-duty aluminum foil before beginning to cook.

SALMON CAVIAR TARTLETS

Poached fresh salmon or canned red salmon may be used in this recipe. If canned, remove any skin before mixing.

6 oz. extra-firm tofu, drained, crumbled

3 tablespoons plain yogurt

3 tablespoons dill sprigs

2 tablespoons fresh lime juice

1/4 teaspoon minced garlic

1/8 teaspoon salt

1/8 teaspoon ground white pepper

1/2 cup flaked, poached or canned salmon

3 tablespoons red salmon caviar

1 (2.1-oz.) pkg. frozen miniature phyllo shells, thawed

1. In food processor, combine tofu, yogurt, dill, lime juice and garlic; process 12 to 15 seconds or until smooth.

2. Transfer mixture to small bowl. Season with salt and pepper.

3. Fold in salmon and 1½ tablespoons caviar. Spoon evenly between shells. Garnish with remaining caviar.

15 tartlets.

Preparation time: 25 minutes.
Ready to serve: 25 minutes.

Per serving: 45 calories, 2 g fat (0.5 g saturated fat), 20 mg cholesterol, 90 mg sodium, 0.5 g fiber.

What is red caviar? Eggs from salmon roe. The eggs are a deep orange or red, and are much less expensive than the black caviar from sturgeon.

All caviar is highly perishable. Store in the refrigerator and use within 2 days of opening.

BREADS

Great bread is no great mystery. All it takes is a little patience, and the right recipe ideas. From muffins to biscuits to sweet breads, and from quick breads to traditional loaves, here are the essential and master recipes you need.

BREADS

Wouldn't it be nice if someone could replicate the aroma of bread coming out of the oven? Here are a variety of great bread recipes to keep your kitchen filled with those heart-warming aromas ... and plates filled with wonderful tastes. You'll find it all here—from classic loaves and basic biscuits to sweeter ideas and fanciful creations.

MUFFINS

2 cups all-purpose flour

3 tablespoons sugar

1/8 teaspoon salt

1 tablespoon baking powder

2 teaspoons grated lemon peel

1 cup milk

1/4 cup vegetable oil

1 egg

❶ Heat oven to 400°F. Spray 12-cup muffin pan with nonstick cooking spray.

❷ In medium bowl, combine flour, sugar, salt, baking powder and lemon peel; mix well. Make a well in center. Whisk in milk, vegetable oil and egg; stir until just moistened. Divide mixture evenly among muffin cups. Sprinkle with cinnamon sugar, if desired.

❸ Bake 20 to 25 minutes or until nicely browned. Let stand in pan 5 minutes; transfer to wire rack. Cool completely.

1 dozen muffins.

Preparation time: 10 minutes.
Ready to serve: 1 hour, 10 minutes.

Per serving: 145 calories, 5.5 g fat (1 g saturated fat), 20 mg cholesterol, 235 mg sodium, 0.5 g fiber.

VARIATION **Chocolate-Melt Muffins**

Insert 1 unwrapped chocolate kiss into batter of each muffin cup before baking.

VARIATION **Macadamia Nut Muffins**

Add 1/2 cup chopped macadamia nuts, 1/4 cup shredded coconut and 1 1/2 teaspoons cardamom to dry ingredients.

VARIATION **Sweet Spice Muffins**

Substitute 3 tablespoons cinnamon sugar and 1/4 teaspoon each ground nutmeg and ground cloves for 3 tablespoons sugar. Brush with warm honey while still hot.

VARIATION **Bacon-Crunch Muffins**

Fold 1/2 cup cooked crumbled bacon into batter.

VARIATION **Cran-Apple Muffins**

Toss 1/2 chopped apple with 2 teaspoons lemon juice. Fold into batter with 1 cup coarsely chopped fresh cranberries. Sprinkle with sugar before baking.

VARIATION **Raisin Bran Muffins**

Fold in 3/4 cup raisins and 1/4 cup crushed bran cereal into batter.

CRAN-APPLE MUFFINS

BISCUITS

Biscuits should be served hot from the oven. The dry ingredients can be combined ahead, covered and refrigerated. Split and toast any leftovers the next day. If you don't have buttermilk, pour 2 teaspoons lemon juice or white vinegar into 1 cup milk. Let stand without stirring 15 minutes at room temperature.

2 cups all-purpose flour
1/2 teaspoon salt
4 teaspoons baking powder
4 tablespoons butter, chilled
1 cup buttermilk

❶ Heat oven to 450°F. Spray baking sheet with nonstick cooking spray.

❷ In medium bowl, combine flour, salt and baking powder. Cut in butter with pastry blender until mixture crumbles.

❸ Make well in center; add enough buttermilk to make soft, slightly sticky dough.

❹ Turn out onto floured surface; pat or roll to 1/2 inch thick. Cut out biscuits with floured 2-inch round cutter. Gather and press remaining dough scraps, continuing until all dough is used.

❺ Arrange biscuits on baking sheet. Bake 10 to 12 minutes or until light brown.

12 to 14 biscuits.

Preparation time: 18 minutes.
Ready to serve: 30 minutes.

Per serving: 120 calories, 4.5 g fat (2.5 g saturated fat), 10 mg cholesterol, 305 mg sodium, 0.5 g fiber.

VARIATION **Berry Shortcake Biscuits**
Add 3 tablespoons sugar to the dry ingredients. Cut into rounds or form 1 large round. Bake large round 15 to 20 minutes. Split while warm. Fill with whipped cream and berries. Top with dollop of whipped cream, whole berries and mint sprigs.

VARIATION **Chive and Cheddar Biscuits**
Stir 3 tablespoons chopped chives and 1/4 cup (1 oz.) grated cheddar cheese into dry ingredients. Sprinkle with paprika before baking.

VARIATION **Sour Cream and Currant Biscuits**
Add 1/4 cup dried currants to dry ingredients. Whisk 3 tablespoons sour cream or sour half-and-half into 3/4 cup milk. Mix into dry ingredients, adding a little more buttermilk as needed to make slightly sticky dough.

VARIATION **Marmalade Biscuits**
With knife, cut 1 teaspoon chunky orange marmalade into each muffin before baking.

Biscuits have become so trendy, multiple interpretations may be found in city and small town bakeries. However, a true biscuit should be dry and fluffy inside with a slightly crisp golden crust, never tough and heavy.

The biscuit preparation method differs from the muffin method in that a solid shortening is cut into the dry ingredients with a pastry blender or with fingers. The consistency is that of coarse crumbs. Liquid ingredients are poured into a well in the center and mixed with a fork, then patted into a round on a floured board.

ALMOND TEA RING

Here, Country-Style White Loaves *(page 60) dough is transformed into an impressive and fancy tea bread. Almond cake filling in a jar may be substituted if you're in a hurry. Add a teaspoon of fresh lemon juice to give a fresh taste.*

BREAD

- 1/3   cup packed brown sugar
- 1/3   cup finely ground almonds
- 1½   tablespoons butter, melted
- 1   tablespoon grated lemon peel
- ½   teaspoon almond extract
- ½   recipe *Country-Style White Loaves* (page 60)

SIMPLE LEMON ICING

- 1   cup powdered sugar
- 1   tablespoon plus 1 teaspoon lemon juice
- 2   tablespoons toasted slivered almonds*

❶ Spray baking sheet with nonstick cooking spray.

❷ In small bowl, combine brown sugar, almonds, 1 tablespoon of the butter, lemon peel and almond extract; mix until paste forms.

❸ Roll dough into 12x7-inch rectangle. Spray dough with nonstick cooking spray. Spread almond filling over dough, and roll up from long side, as for jelly roll. Moisten edges and seam; pinch to seal.

❹ Place, seam side down, on 15x10x1-inch baking sheet. Form into ring and pinch edges together. With scissors, cut V-cuts at 2-inch intervals, without cutting through ring, while twisting each slice slightly onto its side. Brush with remaining ½ tablespoon butter.

❺ Cover and let rise about 45 minutes in draft-free area until doubled.

❻ Heat oven to 375°F. Bake ring 25 minutes or until golden brown. Meanwhile in medium bowl, combine powdered sugar and lemon juice, adding more lemon juice if needed to make smooth icing.

❼ Remove ring from oven; cool on wire rack. Drizzle with Simple Lemon Icing; sprinkle with slivered almonds.

1 (8-slice) tea ring.

Preparation time: 1 hour, 5 minutes.
Ready to serve: 2 hours.

Per serving: 240 calories, 7.5 g fat (3 g saturated fat), 10 mg cholesterol, 165 mg sodium, 1.5 g fiber.

To toast almonds, place on baking sheet; bake at 375°F for 6 minutes or until deep golden brown.

COUNTRY-STYLE WHITE LOAVES

Use a thermometer to eliminate the guesswork from gauging the temperature. If the added liquids are too hot, they will kill the enzymes; if too cold, the yeast will not activate or will do so very slowly. In either case, the bread will not rise properly. This dough may be frozen for up to one month.

5¼ cups all-purpose flour
2 tablespoons sugar
2 (¼-oz.) pkg. active dry yeast
1½ teaspoons salt
2 tablespoons butter
1 cup water
1 cup milk

❶ In large bowl, combine 2 cups of the flour, sugar, yeast and salt. Set aside. In small saucepan, melt 2 tablespoons butter over medium heat. Add water and milk; heat to 110°F to 115°F.

❷ In large bowl, combine flour and butter mixtures; beat 2 minutes at high speed. Add another 1 cup flour; beat an additional 1 to 2 minutes at high speed until smooth. With wooden spoon, stir in enough remaining flour to form soft dough. Turn out onto floured surface. Knead 5 to 8 minutes or until dough is smooth and elastic.

❸ Place in greased bowl, turning to coat all sides of dough. Cover with kitchen towel and set in warm, draft-free area 45 minutes or until doubled.

❹ Heat oven to 400°F. Spray 2 (9x5-inch) loaf pans with nonstick cooking spray.

❺ On floured surface, roll one-half of the dough into 12x7-inch rectangle. Beginning with short end, roll up as for jelly roll. Pinch ends to seal, and place, seam side down, in loaf pan. Repeat with remaining dough. Bake 45 minutes or until crust is golden. Remove from pan immediately. Cool on wire rack.

2 loaves.

Preparation time: 1 hour, 30 minutes.
Ready to serve: 2 hours, 45 minutes.

Per serving: 120 calories, 2 g fat (1 g saturated fat), 5 mg cholesterol, 160 mg sodium, 1 g fiber.

VARIATION **Swirled Cherry Coffeecakes**
Brush each 12x7-inch rectangle with 2 tablespoons melted butter. Sprinkle with 2 teaspoons dried orange peel, ¼ cup crushed, drained pineapple, ¾ cup dried cherries and 1 tablespoon cinnamon sugar. Roll, pinching ends to seal. Place in loaf pans, seam side down.

VARIATION **Granary Bread**
Substitute 3 tablespoons molasses for sugar and beat together with liquid ingredients. Substitute 1½ cups whole-wheat flour for 1½ cups all-purpose flour. Stir in 1¼ cups mixed roasted sunflower seeds, old-fashioned oats and/or toasted wheat germ after the first addition of flour. Before baking, brush with melted butter and sprinkle with 1 tablespoon toasted wheat germ.

Yeast is a live plant. It ferments the sugar and starch in the flour, producing carbon dioxide and ethyl alcohol gases, which cause bread to rise. Dried yeast becomes active when moisture and warmth are added.

To ensure yeast freshness, proper storage is essential. Unopened packages or jars of dry yeast may be kept at room temperature. After opening, store airtight in a refrigerator or freezer and use within four months.

Some recipes still call for compressed yeast, which may be found in the refrigerated section of your supermarket. Two ounces of compressed yeast is equal to 3 (¼-oz.) packages dry yeast.

To freeze dough, divide kneaded dough in half. Flatten each piece to a 6-inch round. Wrap in a 1-gallon resealable plastic bag, squeezing all the air out to make it airtight.

Thaw in the freezer bag (see guidelines on page 61) and allow to rise slightly in the refrigerator, at room temperature or in the microwave. Check often. Thawing times vary according to the temperature of the refrigerator and room. Remove thawed dough from bag; shape, rise and bake as directed.

HOW TO KNEAD BREAD

Everyone should know how to knead bread. Here's how to do it.

- Place dough on lightly floured bread board or pastry cloth.
- Fold dough over toward yourself; press down and away from you with the heel of your hand.
- Give dough a quarter turn and repeat until dough is smooth, elastic and doesn't stick. Most bread should be kneaded for 10 minutes.

Fold dough over and toward yourself.

Press down and away with the heel of your hand.

THAWING GUIDELINES FOR FROZEN BREAD DOUGH	
Refrigerator:	8 to 12 hours
Countertop:	4 to 8 hours
Microwave:	Open bag slightly. Place on a microwave plate or paper plate. Microwave 10 minutes on Low (10%) power, turn over and rotate one quarter turn. Let rest 10 minutes. Repeat once or twice until dough is thawed. Check often during this process.

CORNBREAD

Cornbread is as American as apple pie, but with the distinction of subtle changes in the basic recipe according to region (see variations). Southerners like their cornbread thin and crusty with just a hint of sweetness. Northerners like their cornbread thicker and sweeter, baked with equal quantities of flour and cornmeal. This particular cornbread is Yankee-style, but if desired, you can cut the sugar back to 2 tablespoons.

1	cup milk
2	eggs
1/4	cup butter, melted
1	cup all-purpose flour
1	cup cornmeal
1/4	cup sugar
1	tablespoon baking powder
1/2	teaspoon salt

❶ Heat oven to 425°F. Spray 8-inch square pan with nonstick cooking spray.

❷ In medium bowl, whisk together milk, eggs and butter. With fork, stir in flour, cornmeal, sugar, baking powder and salt just until moistened.

❸ Pour into pan. Bake 20 to 25 minutes or until golden and toothpick inserted near center comes out clean.

❹ Cut into squares. Serve hot with unsalted butter.

12 servings.

Preparation time: 10 minutes.
Ready to serve: 35 minutes.

Per serving: 155 calories, 5.5 g fat (3 g saturated fat), 50 mg cholesterol, 265 mg sodium, 1 g fiber.

VARIATION **Golden Kernel Cornbread**
Add 1 cup fresh or thawed frozen corn to the dry ingredients.

VARIATION **Mexican Cornbread**
Fold 1 (4-oz.) can drained, chopped green chiles and 1/2 cup (2 oz.) grated cheddar cheese into batter.

VARIATION **Cornbread with Scallions and Peppers**
Add 1 thinly sliced scallion, 1/4 cup chopped red bell pepper and 3/4 teaspoon crushed fresh sage to the wet ingredients.

VARIATION **Tomato-Dill Cornbread**
Add 1/3 cup chopped sun-dried tomatoes and 2 tablespoons chopped fresh dill to dry ingredients.

DARK STICKY GINGERBREAD

This fluffy, moist and dark quick bread includes diced crystallized ginger and powdered ginger, both of which pack a powerful punch.

GINGERBREAD

- 1 cup packed brown sugar
- 1 cup unsalted butter, softened
- ¾ cup plus 2 tablespoons dark molasses
- 2 eggs
- ⅓ cup milk
- 1⅔ cups all-purpose flour
- 1 teaspoon baking soda
- 1 rounded tablespoon ground ginger
- 2 teaspoons cinnamon
- ½ teaspoon freshly ground pepper
- ¼ cup chopped crystallized ginger

WHISKEY CREAM

- 2 tablespoons whiskey or bourbon
- 1 cup heavy cream, whipped
  Dash ground ginger

❶ Heat oven to 325°F. Spray 11x7-inch baking dish with nonstick cooking spray. Set aside.

❷ In medium bowl, beat brown sugar and butter at medium speed until light and fluffy. Add ¾ cup of the molasses, eggs, milk and ⅔ cup of the flour. Beat until smooth.

❸ Gradually stir in remaining 1 cup flour, adding baking soda, spices and pepper. Fold in crystallized ginger.

❹ Pour into baking dish. Bake 30 to 35 minutes or until toothpick inserted near center comes out clean. Center will fall slightly. While hot, brush with remaining 2 tablespoons molasses. Cool before cutting into squares.

❺ To prepare cream, fold whiskey gently into whipped cream. Swirl one spoonful on each serving of gingerbread, and dust very lightly with ground ginger. Refrigerate leftover cream.

1 (11x7-inch) cake.

Preparation time: 20 minutes.
Ready to serve: 1 hour, 30 minutes.

Per serving: 295 calories, 15 g fat (9 g saturated fat), 65 mg cholesterol, 115 mg sodium, 0.5 g fiber.

This bread actually improves with age!

Wrap tightly in parchment paper, then plastic wrap and refrigerate up to 2 weeks. You can also bake this bread in 2 (9-inch) pie pans and cut into wedges. Serve one and freeze the other. Delicious with coffee or as a warm dessert topped with ice cream.

SOUR CREAM POPPY SEED ROLL

A rich yeast crust blends with its orange-scented poppy seed filling to make this coffee cake a winner. Prepared poppy seed cake filling is available in the baking section of your supermarket. Enhance the filling with finely chopped orange peel and freshly grated ginger. The roll freezes well.

1	(12-oz.) jar poppy seed cake filling
1/4	cup dried currants
3	tablespoons finely chopped orange peel
1	tablespoon grated fresh ginger
1	(1/4-oz.) pkg. active dry yeast
1/4	cup warm water (110°F to 115°F)
3	tablespoons honey, warmed
1/2	cup butter
1/2	cup reduced-fat sour cream
1/2	teaspoon salt
3	cups all-purpose flour
2	eggs

❶ Heat oven to at 350°F. Spray large baking sheet with nonstick cooking spray.

❷ In small bowl, mix poppy seed filling, currants, orange peel and ginger. Set aside. In large cup, sprinkle yeast over warm water. Add 1 tablespoon of the honey. Do not stir. Set aside. In large saucepan, melt butter. Add remaining 2 tablespoons honey, sour cream and salt. Heat to 120°F to 125°F.

❸ Pour into large bowl; stir in 1 cup of the flour. Add eggs and yeast mixture; beat at medium speed until smooth. Add enough of the remaining 2 cups flour to make soft dough. Turn out onto floured surface. Knead 3 to 4 minutes or until smooth and elastic, adding more flour as needed to keep from sticking. Form dough into ball; cover with kitchen towel and let rest 10 minutes.

❹ Roll one half of the dough into 12x8-inch rectangle. Spread with one-half of the poppy seed mixture. Starting from long side, roll up as for jelly roll. Moisten edges and ends with a little water; pinch to seal.

❺ Place, seam side down, on baking sheet. Repeat with remaining dough and filling. Cover with kitchen towel. Let rise in draft-free area about 1 hour or until doubled.

❻ Bake 30 minutes or until golden brown. Cool completely on wire rack. Sprinkle with sugar, if desired. Diagonally slice to serve.

2 rolls.

Preparation time: 2 hours.
Ready to serve: 3 hours.

Per serving: 250 calories, 9 g fat (4 g saturated fat), 45 mg cholesterol, 105 mg sodium, 2 g fiber.

HARVEST LOAF

This loaf offers the fragrance of autumn and the texture of a cake. Feel free to substitute dried cranberries for fresh, so that this loaf could be a year-round favorite. Cool the loaf completely before slicing thickly with a serrated knife. Harvest Loaf is absolutely grand at breakfast, toasted and slathered with butter or honey.

BREAD

1/2	cup butter, softened
1 1/2	cups sugar
2	eggs
1 2/3	cups all-purpose flour
1	cup canned pumpkin
1 1/2	teaspoons baking powder
2 1/2	teaspoons pumpkin pie spice
1/3	cup milk
1/2	cup chopped hazelnuts
3/4	cup coarsely chopped cranberries
1/4	teaspoon salt

NUTMEG CREAM GLAZE

1	cup powdered sugar, sifted
	Dash ground nutmeg
1	teaspoon butter, melted
1 to 2	tablespoons heavy cream, whipped

❶ Heat oven to 350°F. Spray 9x5-inch loaf pan with nonstick cooking spray.

❷ In medium bowl, beat butter and sugar at medium speed until blended. Add eggs with 2 tablespoons of the flour; beat well. Add pumpkin; stir to blend.

❸ Mix remaining flour with baking powder and pumpkin pie spice. Add alternately with milk, beating well after each addition. Stir in hazelnuts, cranberries and salt.

❹ Spoon batter into pan, spreading smoothly. Bake 1 hour or until toothpick inserted near center comes out clean.

❺ Cool in pan 10 minutes. Loosen sides with spatula; turn out onto wire rack to cool.

❻ To prepare Nutmeg Cream Glaze, combine powdered sugar and nutmeg with butter and cream. Drizzle over cooled bread.

1 loaf.

Preparation time: 20 minutes.
Ready to serve: 2 hours and 10 minutes.

Per serving: 330 calories, 13 g fat (6 g saturated fat), 60 mg cholesterol, 130 mg sodium, 2 g fiber.

BREAKFAST & BRUNCH

On the culinary scene, brunch gets little attention at all. Pure breakfast gets even less press. But sooner or later you're going to have occasions—whether company's in the house or not—when you'll want to treat everybody to wonderful dishes like these.

BREAKFAST & BRUNCH

The words "involved," "timely" and "complex" never seem to jibe with the eating occasions of breakfast and brunch. But you can still eat great food. The essential and master recipes that follow are proof.

ESSENTIAL

CLASSIC OMELET

2 large eggs
2 tablespoons cold water
Dash salt
Dash ground white pepper
2 teaspoons unsalted butter

❶ In small bowl, whisk together eggs, water, salt and pepper until well blended.

❷ In small nonstick skillet, melt 2 teaspoons butter over medium-high heat. Pour in egg mixture.

❸ Using wide spatula and working from edges, push cooked mixture gently towards center. Tilt skillet so uncooked mixture flows towards edges to cook. Shake pan back and forth frequently.

❹ When surface is set, add filling of your choice. Fold omelet over, and slide onto warm plate. Serve immediately.

1 omelet.

Preparation time: 5 minutes.
Ready to serve: 10 minutes.

Per serving: 215 calories, 17.5 g fat (8 g saturated fat), 445 mg cholesterol, 405 mg sodium, 0 g fiber.

VARIATION **Herb and Cheddar Omelet**
Sprinkle 2 tablespoons finely chopped fresh herbs (such as parsley, tarragon and basil) and 2 tablespoons shredded cheddar cheese on omelet before folding over.

VARIATION **Chicken Liver Omelet**
Before serving, top omelet with combined 1/4 cup chopped cooked chicken livers, 1 tablespoon sour cream and 1/4 teaspoon dried marjoram.

VARIATION **Sour Cream and Caviar Omelet**
Top omelet with 2 tablespoons sour cream and sprinkle 2 teaspoons caviar over. Garnish with dollop of sour cream and caviar.

VARIATION **Blueberry-Peach Omelet**
Toss 1/4 cup blueberries with 2 tablespoons warm peach preserves. Spoon over half of omelet before folding over.

VARIATION **Sweet Cinnamon Raisin Omelet**
Combine 1 tablespoon sugar with 1/8 teaspoon cinnamon and 2 tablespoons golden raisins. Reserve 2 teaspoons mixture. Sprinkle remaining mixture over omelet. Fold over and sprinkle reserved cinnamon raisins on top.

Omelet pans are shallow with sloping sides so that the omelet can slide out easily with a little help from a wide spatula. Omelets may be filled with sweet or savory mixtures using 1/4 to 1/3 cup filling for each two-egg omelet. Spoon filling on top of omelet before folding it over.

To make a sweet omelet, substitute 1/4 teaspoon sugar for the salt and pepper. If you prepare fillings ahead of time, you can make omelets from start to finish in less than 3 minutes.

To avoid a greenish tinge when held for a short time, place cooked eggs over pan of hot water rather than over direct heat.

Never add raw eggs to cooked eggs to "refresh" them.

FRENCH TOAST

French toast is simply thick slices of bread soaked in an egg mixture. The variations make it divine. Any type of bread may be used, but I prefer egg bread (challah), which when cooked becomes crusty on the outside with a fluffy, moist interior.

4	eggs
3/4	cup milk
1	tablespoon sugar
3/4	teaspoon vanilla
4	(3/4-inch) slices challah or other bread
1 1/2	tablespoons vegetable oil

❶ In large shallow dish, whisk together eggs, milk, sugar and vanilla.

❷ Arrange slices in one layer in mixture. Let soak 2 to 3 minutes per side.

❸ Heat oil in large skillet over high heat until hot. Transfer soaked bread to skillet. Reduce heat to medium.

❹ Cook about 3 to 4 minutes per side, until cooked through and nicely browned.

❺ Serve hot, dusted with powdered sugar, if desired.

4 servings.
Preparation time: 15 minutes.
Ready to serve: 25 minutes.

Per serving: 235 calories, 11 g fat (3 g saturated fat), 230 mg cholesterol, 145 mg sodium, 0.5 g fiber.

VARIATION **Baked French Toast**
Heat oven to 500°F. Sprinkle both sides of egg-soaked bread with finely ground almonds. Place on generously buttered or oiled baking sheet. Bake 5 to 6 minutes until underside is golden brown. Flip over. Top each slice with 1 teaspoon butter or brush or spray generously with vegetable oil. Bake an additional 4 to 5 minutes or until golden brown and no uncooked egg mixture remains. May be topped with preserves, fruit compote or maple syrup.

VARIATION **Apricot-Stuffed French Toast**
In large bowl, combine 1/2 cup softened cream cheese, 2 tablespoons finely chopped dried apricots and 1 tablespoon apricot preserves. Spread mixture evenly over 4 slices bread. Top each slice with another bread slice. Soak in egg mixture and fry.

VARIATION **Sticky Bun Baked French Toast**
Cut sticky buns into thirds horizontally. Place in greased 9-inch square dish. Pour egg mixture over buns. Let soak 4 to 6 hours or overnight before baking.

Day-old bread or muffins are perfect for French toast. It is said that frugal New Orleans cooks developed this breakfast dish to use up stale breads that otherwise would have been discarded.

If very thick bread slices are used, make sure that they are cooked through. Internal temperature should reach at least 160°F.

BLUEBERRY-GINGER PANCAKES

PANCAKES

Even the best mixes can't compare to pancakes made the old-fashioned way and eaten hot from the skillet. If you don't have buttermilk, add 2 teaspoons lemon juice or white vinegar to 1 cup milk and let stand at room temperature for 5 minutes without stirring.

1	cup all-purpose flour
2	teaspoons sugar
1½	teaspoons baking powder
½	teaspoon salt
1	egg
1	cup buttermilk
3	tablespoons vegetable oil

❶ In medium bowl, stir together flour, sugar, baking powder and salt.

❷ Make well in center. Add egg, buttermilk and 1 tablespoon of the oil; whisk until smooth.

❸ Pour remaining 2 tablespoons oil into large skillet. Heat over medium-high heat until hot.

❹ Pour scant ¼ cup batter into skillet. When bubbles appear and burst on surface, flip over and continue cooking about 1 to 2 minutes until underside is golden brown.

❺ Serve hot with sweet butter and maple or fruit syrups, if desired.

15 (3-inch) pancakes.

Preparation time: 15 minutes.
Ready to serve: 25 minutes.

Per serving: 105 calories, 5 g fat (1 g saturated fat), 25 mg cholesterol, 215 mg sodium, 0.5 g fiber.

VARIATION **Apple-Raisin Pancakes**
Fold 1 unpeeled chopped apple and ¼ cup raisins into batter.

VARIATION **Blueberry-Ginger Pancakes**
Toss 1 cup blueberries with ½ teaspoon ground ginger; fold into batter.

VARIATION **Pineapple-Walnut Pancakes**
Combine ¼ cup drained crushed pineapple with ⅓ cup chopped walnuts; fold into batter.

VARIATION **Crisp Bacon Pancakes**
Omit sugar; stir ½ cup crumbled crisp cooked bacon into batter.

VARIATION **Southern Cornmeal Pancakes**
Omit sugar, decrease flour to ½ cup and add ½ cup cornmeal; fold in ½ cup cooked or canned corn to batter.

VARIATION **Cheddar Cheese Pancakes**
Omit sugar; stir 1 cup (4 oz.) shredded cheddar cheese and 1 teaspoon dried parsley into batter.

For speed and ease, combine the dry ingredients for 4 recipes of pancakes. Store in an air-tight container in a cool, dry place—not the refrigerator. When needed, add wet ingredients for 1 recipe (1 cup buttermilk plus 3 tablespoons vegetable oil) to 1 cup plus 1 tablespoon of the dry mixture.

PERFECTLY COOKED SCRAMBLED EGGS

Americans adore scrambled eggs: they are the most popular items on restaurant menus. Scrambled eggs should be light with fluffy, creamy curds. If they're dry, the eggs have been cooked over high heat. The secrets are energetic beating, cooking over medium heat and gentle stirring.

    4   eggs
    3   tablespoons water
    2   tablespoons reduced-fat milk
        Dash salt
        Dash ground white pepper
    1   tablespoon plus 1 teaspoon
            unsalted butter

❶ In small bowl, whisk together eggs, water, milk, salt and pepper.

❷ In medium skillet, melt butter over medium heat; pour in egg mixture.

❸ Stir bottom and sides of skillet with spatula 5 minutes or until large, creamy curds form.

❹ Continue cooking only until eggs are still slightly moist. Remove from heat immediately while turning over once or twice with spatula. Spoon onto warm plates. Sprinkle with parsley, if desired.

2 servings.

Preparation time: 5 minutes.
Ready to serve: 12 minutes.

Per serving: 225 calories, 18 g fat (8 g saturated fat), 445 mg cholesterol, 275 mg sodium, 0 g fiber.

YANKEE KEDGEREE

Kedgeree is a popular British breakfast dish, a recipe brought back by employees of the East India company. It is a soft, creamy mixture of curried rice and smoked fish. Black beans, pimento, celery and tuna add a distinctive New World touch to this recipe.

    2   hard-cooked eggs, halved
    3   tablespoons vegetable oil
    1   medium onion, finely chopped
    2   cups cooked long-grain rice
    1   (12-oz.) can white tuna, drained, flaked*
    1   tablespoon curry powder
    1/3   cup chopped pimento
    1/2   cup canned black beans, rinsed
    1/8   teaspoon salt

❶ Sieve egg yolks. Chop egg whites coarsely; set aside.

❷ In large saucepan, heat oil over medium heat. Sauté onion 3 to 4 minutes or until softened. Remove from heat.

❸ Stir in rice, tuna, curry powder, pimento, beans and egg whites. Season with salt.

❹ Spoon onto warm platter. Garnish with egg yolk. Serve warm.

TIP *Tiny cooked shrimp or other cooked seafood could be substituted for tuna.

4 to 6 servings.

Preparation time: 25 minutes.
Ready to serve: 35 minutes.

Per serving: 380 calories, 14 g fat (2.5 g saturated fat), 130 mg cholesterol, 1015 mg sodium, 3 g fiber.

"TO HEALTH" BIRCHERMUESLI

Though the traditional dish is made of uncooked oatmeal soaked in water and mixed with thick, sweet, condensed milk, I like to toast the oatmeal for a crunchier, chewy texture. In summer, berries and other seasonal fruits may be used instead of dried fruits.

2 cups old-fashioned or quick-cooking oats
1/4 cup wheat germ
1/2 teaspoon cinnamon
1 unpeeled Granny Smith apple, chopped
1 cup chopped mixed dried fruits*
2 tablespoons chopped slivered almonds
1 cup half-and-half
1 tablespoon honey, warmed

❶ Spread oatmeal on baking sheet. Toast under broiler about 2 to 3 minutes or until golden brown. Transfer to large bowl.

❷ Stir in one-half of the wheat germ, cinnamon, apple, dried fruits and almonds.

❸ In separate bowl, combine half-and-half and honey; mix well. Pour over oatmeal mixture; stir gently to mix. Sprinkle remaining wheat germ on top.

TIP *Substitute 1 cup berries for dried fruits. Reserve a few berries for garnish, if desired.

4 to 6 servings.
Preparation time: 10 minutes.
Ready to serve: 20 minutes.

Per serving: 420 calories, 12.5 g fat (5 g saturated fat), 25 mg cholesterol, 30 mg sodium, 9 g fiber.

Birchermuesli was served to patients at the Zurich clinic owned and operated by Swiss Doctor R. Bircher-Benner. A progressive physician and nutritionist, he was convinced that fresh fruits, vegetables and grains were healthier than the starchy diet of the early 20th century. Today, Birchermuesli is a staple dish served in Swiss homes and restaurants.

BREAKFAST POPOVER

Sausages, vegetables, puffy popover—an all-in-one dish perfect for a weekend brunch or breakfast. Vegetables may be substituted, if desired.

- 1 (7-oz.) pkg. brown-and-serve sausages
- 2 medium portobello mushrooms, sliced
- 1/2 red bell pepper, thinly sliced
- 1 scallion, thinly sliced
- 2 eggs
- 1 tablespoon vegetable oil
- 1 cup milk
- 1 cup all-purpose flour
- 1 tablespoon fresh sage or 1 teaspoon dried
- 2 to 3 drops hot pepper sauce
- 1/4 teaspoon salt
- 1/4 cup (1 oz.) shredded sharp cheddar cheese

❶ Heat oven to 400°F. Spray 9-inch square pan with nonstick cooking spray.

❷ Cut each sausage into thirds. Place sausages in pan. Arrange mushrooms, bell pepper and scallion over sausages. Bake 4 minutes.

❸ In blender, combine eggs, oil, milk, flour, sage, hot pepper sauce and salt; blend 20 seconds at high speed until mixture is set.

❹ Pour egg mixture over mushroom mixture. Sprinkle with cheese; return to oven. Bake 20 to 25 minutes or until browned. Serve immediately.

4 to 6 servings.

Preparation time: 15 minutes.
Ready to serve: 45 minutes.

Per serving: 410 calories, 24 g fat (9.5 g saturated fat), 149 mg cholesterol, 620 mg sodium, 1.5 g fiber.

SMOKED SALMON AND OLIVE QUICHE

The savory egg-cheese pie hails from the Alsace-Lorraine region of France. The popular Quiche Lorraine is a pastry shell with crisp bacon bits folded into a savory custard filling before baking. Almost any vegetables and/or meats may be used as in this version. Make a couple quiches. Enjoy one and freeze the other.

- 1 (9-inch) unbaked pie shell
- 6 (1-oz.) slices *Sima's Gravlax* (page 48)
- 3 tablespoons chopped ripe olives
- 2 to 3 tablespoons capers, rinsed
- 3 eggs
- 1 cup milk
- 2 tablespoons sour cream
  Dash ground white pepper

❶ Heat oven to 350°F.

❷ Prick bottom and sides of pie shell with fork. Bake 5 minutes.

❸ Place 1 1/2 teaspoons chopped olives on each salmon slice. Roll up as for jelly roll. Arrange in wagon wheel pattern on bottom of pie shell. Sprinkle with capers.

❹ In medium bowl, whisk eggs, milk, sour cream and pepper. Pour over salmon.

❺ Place on baking sheet. Bake 45 minutes or until toothpick inserted near center comes out clean. Serve warm or at room temperature.

6 servings.

Preparation time: 20 minutes.
Ready to serve: 1 hour, 5 minutes.

Per serving: 165 calories, 10 g fat (3 g saturated fat), 95 mg cholesterol, 290 mg sodium, 0.5 g fiber.

VARIATION **Tomato and Roasted Garlic Quiche**
Add 2 chopped tomatoes and 1/2 cup shredded roasted garlic cheddar cheese to egg mixture. Bake as directed above.

SMOKED SALMON AND OLIVE QUICHE

PINEAPPLE AND BROWN SUGAR STRATA

Easy and fuss-free, this is a much requested brunch dish at our house. It may be assembled the night before, covered and refrigerated. Then 45 minutes before serving, slip into a preheated oven and bake as directed below.

½ cup butter

1 cup packed brown sugar

1 (20-oz.) can crushed pineapple, drained, juice reserved

4 eggs

3 sourdough English muffins, torn into 1-inch pieces

½ cup old-fashioned or quick-cooking oats

2 tablespoons grated orange peel

❶ Heat oven to 375°F.

❷ In large bowl, beat 6 tablespoons butter and ¾ cup of the brown sugar at medium speed until fluffy. Spread mixture over bottom of 9-inch deep dish pie pan.

❸ Spread pineapple over brown sugar mixture. Set aside.

❹ In another large bowl, whisk together eggs and reserved pineapple juice. Add sourdough muffin pieces; press down to soak. Pour over crushed pineapple.

❺ In small bowl, cut oatmeal, orange peel and remaining ¼ cup brown sugar into remaining 2 tablespoons butter until mixture crumbles. Sprinkle over pie.

❻ Bake 40 minutes or until bubbly at sides. Serve warm.

8 servings.

Preparation time: 25 minutes.
Ready to serve: 1 hour, 5 minutes.

Per serving: 355 calories, 15 g fat (8 g saturated fat), 135 mg cholesterol, 220 mg sodium, 1.5 g fiber.

FISH & SEAFOOD

Good, fresh fish and seafood is never really easy or cheap to obtain, yet the taste is always worth the effort and dollars. The final piece to the puzzle is preparing your "catch" in a way that will celebrate its flavor and make it the star. Here are the recipe ideas you need to do just that.

FISH & SEAFOOD

Fish and seafood are the most perishable of our fresh foods. They are also one of nature's fast foods—cooked and ready to eat in minutes.

There are two main groups of fish and seafood: fin fish are those with fins and vertebrae, such as flounder, salmon and trout. Shellfish are aquatic crustaceans, such as shrimp, lobster and crab.

To increase availability, much of our fish and seafood is farmed, but prices are still high. To avoid waste, and really appreciate the extraordinary flavors and varied textures, fish must be properly purchased and cooked. Here are a few guidelines in those respects.

FRESH FISH

Fresh fish should be displayed on ice, usually behind a glass counter. There are a couple of freshness points you can check: the eyes should be clear, not milky or sunken, and gills should be reddish-pink. You won't be able to smell or check the fish in the store, but when you get outside or home, check that the flesh is firm when pressed with your finger. Also give it the best test of all—smell it. Fish should never smell truly "fishy." In fact, there should be absolutely no odor at all. If so, take it back and get a refund. Smelly fish is not fresh, and when cooked the fishy odor will intensify and fill your kitchen with the most unappetizing odors.

PACKAGED FISH

Packaged frozen fish should be solid with no discoloration or freezer burn. Choose fish in tightly wrapped packages with no tears or open ends. There should be no odor when frozen or thawed.

COOKING FISH

The rule of thumb for fish cookery is 10 minutes per 1 inch of thickness. Seafood, such as scallops and shrimp, may be cooked in less than 5 minutes depending on size and cooking method. Raw fish is edible, as in pickled herring and gravlax.

The microwave is an indispensable kitchen appliance, but it's as quick—if not quicker—to cook fish on the stovetop or under the broiler.

PLAIN BOILED SHRIMP

Shrimp may be cooked fresh or frozen. They might already be deveined when you purchase them. If not, remove the dark vein down the middle of the back by making a shallow cut with a small, sharp-pointed knife, then wash out under cold running water.

1 1/2 quarts water
1 teaspoon peppercorns
2 teaspoons kosher (coarse) salt
1 to 2 lb. shelled, deveined uncooked
   medium shrimp*

1. In large pot, bring water, peppercorns and salt to a rolling boil over high heat.

2. Add shrimp; return to a boil. Cover and reduce heat to a simmer.

3. Cook 3 minutes or just until shrimp turn pink. If frozen, cook an additional 1 to 2 minutes. Drain; cool.

TIP *An approximate count per pound of shrimp with shells is 10 to 12 jumbo, 15 to 20 large, 26 to 30 medium and 40 to 45 small.

4 servings.
Preparation time: 5 minutes.
Ready to serve: 10 minutes.

Per serving: 80 calories, 1 g fat (0 g saturated fat), 160 mg cholesterol, 455 mg sodium, 0 g fiber.

VARIATION **Shrimp in Beer**
In large saucepan, combine 2 (12-oz.) cans beer, 1 tablespoon seafood seasoning and 2 teaspoons salt. Bring to a boil. Add 1 1/2 lb. unpeeled shrimp. Simmer, covered, 3 to 5 minutes or until shrimp are firm and pink. Drain well and serve with melted butter and splash of lemon juice.

BROILED FLOUNDER FILLETS

Any fish fillet—such as sole, red snapper, tilapia, walleye or shad—can be cooked using this method as long as the fillet is less than 3/4 inch thick. Just slip the fillet under a preheated broiler and cook 5 minutes per 1/2 inch of thickness. No need to turn.

4 (about 1 1/4-lb.) flounder fillets
2 to 3 tablespoons vegetable oil
1/8 teaspoon salt
1/8 teaspoon lemon-pepper seasoning

1. Heat broiler. Line baking sheet with aluminum foil and spray with nonstick cooking spray.

2. Rinse fillets under cold water and pat dry. Place on baking sheet; brush generously with vegetable oil. Sprinkle lightly with salt and lemon-pepper seasoning.

3. Place under broiler about 4 inches from heat. Cook 5 minutes or until fillets flake easily with fork. Garnish with parsley sprigs and one lemon wedge on the side.

4 servings.
Preparation time: 5 minutes.
Ready to serve: 10 minutes.

Per serving: 210 calories, 9 g fat (1.5 g saturated fat), 90 mg cholesterol, 215 mg sodium, 0 g fiber.

VARIATION **Lemon-Garlic Butter**
Blend 2 teaspoons grated lemon peel and 1/2 teaspoon garlic powder into 4 tablespoons softened unsalted butter. Shape into log about 1 inch thick. Chill. Top hot cooked fillets with a pat of Lemon-Garlic butter.

VARIATION **Sun-Dried Tomato Sauce**
Whisk 1 tablespoon each finely chopped sun-dried tomatoes and chopped chives into 4 tablespoons vinaigrette dressing. Drizzle over cooked fish before serving.

To test for doneness, fish should be opaque when flakes are separated with a fork. If a white curd appears between flakes, fish is overcooked.

SAUTEED SCALLOPS

Scallops may be small, as in small bay scallops (about ¹/₂ inch in diameter) and larger, as in sea scallops (about 1¹/₂ to 2 inches in diameter). Either way, this is a delicious and simple way to prepare them.

    3   tablespoons olive oil
    1   lb. scallops
    1   tablespoon butter
    1   tablespoon chopped garlic
    2   small shallots, chopped

1. Heat olive oil in large skillet over medium-high heat until hot. Cook scallops quickly, stirring constantly about 3 to 5 minutes or until opaque. Transfer to warm platter.

2. In large skillet, melt butter over medium heat. Sauté garlic and shallots 3 to 4 minutes or until golden. Pour sauce over scallops. Garnish with lemon slices and parsley. Serve immediately.

4 servings.
Preparation time: 10 minutes.
Ready to serve: 20 minutes.

Per serving: 250 calories, 14.5 g fat (3.5 g saturated fat), 45 mg cholesterol, 320 mg sodium, 0.5 g fiber.

Fresh scallops should be pale and translucent with no discoloration. They are versatile in that they may be cooked in a variety of methods: sautéed, broiled, fried, poached or grilled.

Before cooking, rinse scallops in cold water and pat dry. Do not overcook or scallops become tough, chewy and unpleasant to eat. When cooked, scallop meat is creamy white with a silky texture.

POACHED SALMON STEAKS

Use a large skillet with a lid for poaching thick fish steaks, such as salmon or tuna. When cooked, a wide fish spatula makes it easy to transfer from skillet to platter. Equal quantities of court bouillon (brought to boil) and boiling water may be used for poaching instead of the liquids below.

    4   (8-oz.) salmon steaks, about 1 inch thick
         Boiling water
    2   tablespoons fresh lemon juice
    2   bay leaves

1. Spray large skillet with nonstick cooking spray. Arrange steaks in skillet in one layer.

2. Pour enough boiling water over fish to come half way up sides of steaks. Pour lemon juice over fish; tuck bay leaves under fish.

3. Bring to a simmer over medium heat. Cover and cook 8 to 10 minutes or until fish flakes easily with fork.

4. Use wide, slotted spatula to remove fish from skillet. Drain on paper towels. Discard bay leaves.

5. Serve hot or chilled garnished with lemon wedges, Dilled Mayonnaise or Speedy Provencale, if desired.

4 servings.
Preparation time: 5 minutes.
Ready to serve: 15 minutes.

Per serving: 170 calories, 7 g fat (2 g saturated fat), 80 mg cholesterol, 70 mg sodium, 0 g fiber.

VARIATION **Dilled Mayonnaise Sauce**
In large bowl, combine ³/₄ cup mayonnaise with ¹/₄ cup plain yogurt and 2 tablespoons fresh dill. Season with ground white pepper. Store covered in refrigerator.

VARIATION **Provencale Sauce**
Stir 2 tablespoons chopped roasted red bell peppers and 2 tablespoons chopped niçoise olives into 1 cup drained chopped Italian-style tomatoes. Store covered in refrigerator.

POACHED SALMON STEAKS

STUFFED TROUT IN RED WINE SAUCE

A pan-dressed fish is one that is scaled and gutted with the head and fins removed. All that needs to be done before cooking: rinse thoroughly in cold water. A heavy, 12-inch skillet will comfortably hold 4 (8-oz. each) whole pan-dressed trout.

TROUT

1	red onion, cut into 1-inch chunks
3	large shallots, quartered
1/2	cup seasoned croutons
1/2	cup cilantro sprigs
4	tablespoons butter
1/4	cup all-purpose flour
1	rounded tablespoon sweet paprika
4	(8-oz.) trout, pan-dressed

SAUCE

1/2	cup red wine
1/4	cup fish stock or water
1/8	teaspoon salt
1/8	teaspoon freshly ground pepper

❶ In food processor, coarsely chop onion, shallots, croutons and cilantro.

❷ In large nonstick skillet, melt 1 tablespoon of the butter over medium heat. Sauté onion mixture about 5 minutes or until onions begin to soften. Set aside.

❸ In large bowl, combine flour and paprika. Place trout in casserole; turn to coat with flour mixture. Shake off excess flour. Spoon onion mixture into cavity of each trout.

❹ Heat remaining 3 tablespoons butter in skillet over medium-high heat. Fry trout 3 to 4 minutes per side until nicely browned.

❺ In small bowl, combine wine and fish stock; pour into pan. Season with salt and pepper. Partially cover; simmer 10 minutes or until fish flakes easily with fork. Transfer to heated platter and keep warm. Cook sauce until reduced and slightly thickened; drizzle over trout.

4 servings.

Preparation time: 20 minutes.
Ready to serve: 50 minutes.

Per serving: 465 calories, 25 g fat (9.5 g saturated fat), 145 mg cholesterol, 315 mg sodium, 2 g fiber.

RED SNAPPER STEW

Any white-fleshed fillets, such as perch, scrod, flounder or whiting, may be substituted for red snapper here. If you don't have pesto, stir in chopped fresh or dried parsley before serving.

1	tablespoon vegetable oil
1	cup frozen baby onions
1	cup unpeeled diced Yukon Gold potatoes
1/2	cup coarsely chopped fennel
1/2	cup fresh or frozen corn, thawed
1	(8-oz.) can clam juice
1	(14.5-oz.) can Italian-style chopped tomatoes
1	(10-oz.) can whole baby clams
1	teaspoon seafood seasoning
1	(8-oz.) red snapper fillet, cut into 1-inch pieces
1	rounded tablespoon *Fresh Herb Pesto* (page 50)

1. In medium saucepan, heat oil over medium heat until hot. Stir in onions, potatoes and fennel; cook, stirring often, 5 minutes.

2. Add corn, clam juice, chopped tomatoes, clams and seasoning. Bring to a simmer. Add red snapper. Cook 5 minutes or until cooked through.

3. Stir in Fresh Herb Pesto; adjust seasoning. Serve hot.

4 to 6 servings.

Preparation time: 15 minutes.
Ready to serve: 30 minutes.

Per serving: 320 calories, 9 g fat (1.5 g saturated fat), 80 mg cholesterol, 575 mg sodium, 3 g fiber.

BRAISED CHILEAN SEA BASS

Large and thick steaks, such as halibut or tuna, may also be used for this dish. It may be prepared and refrigerated up to 12 hours ahead of mealtime. Add Court Bouillon *(page 160) or lemon water before placing in the oven.*

2	cups mixed fresh green herbs
3/4	cup sun-dried tomatoes, cut into 3/4-inch chunks
2	scallions, cut into 2-inch pieces
1	teaspoon chopped garlic
1/4	cup dry vermouth
	Scant 1/4 cup olive oil
4	(1 1/2-lb.) Chilean sea bass fillets
2	tablespoons dry bread crumbs
1/4 to 1/2	cup *Court Bouillon* (page 160) or lemon water*

1 Heat oven to 425°F.

2 In food processor, coarsely chop herbs, tomatoes, scallions and garlic; pour in vermouth and 2 tablespoons olive oil.

3 Spread one-half of the herb mixture over bottom of 3-quart casserole. Top with fish; press remaining herb mixture on fish. Drizzle with remaining oil; sprinkle with seasoned bread crumbs. Pour 1/4 cup bouillon into casserole.

4 Bake 10 minutes or until topping is golden, adding more liquid, if needed. Cover tightly with aluminum foil.

5 Reduce heat to 375°F. Cook an additional 15 to 20 minutes or until fish is opaque and flakes easily with fork.

TIP *Lemon water is a simple mixture of 1 tablespoon lemon juice added to 1/2 cup water.

4 servings.

Preparation time: 15 minutes.
Ready to serve: 45 minutes.

Per serving: 315 calories, 16 g fat (2.5 g saturated fat), 80 mg cholesterol, 405 mg sodium, 3 g fiber.

VARIATION **Crisp-Skinned Chilean Sea Bass**

Remove as much water as possible from skin of 4 fish steaks by drawing back of knife blade firmly back and forth over fish like windshield wiper. Continue until no more water appears. Season both sides with salt and freshly ground pepper. Heat about 1/8 inch vegetable oil in skillet over high heat. Cook fish, skin side down, and reduce heat to medium. Press to flatten; cook 3 to 4 minutes or until skin is crisp. Turn and cook an additional 4 to 5 minutes or until fish flakes easily with fork. Serve with chutney or salsa.

Patagonian toothfish is marketed as Chilean sea bass. It is slow-growing and found in the deep, cold waters in the Southern Hemisphere, particularly Antarctica. The fish is high in fat with a mild, white flaky flesh. Chilean sea bass became commercially available in the U.S. in 1991. Since then, thanks to creative chefs, it has become enormously popular. So that this fish does not get fished out, harvesting is regulated by the Conference for the Conservation of Antarctic Marine Living Resources, and all Chilean sea bass imported into the U.S. is monitored through the National Marine Fisheries Service.

BLACKENED PERCH FILLETS

Paul Prudhomme, the New Orleans chef, is famous for his Blackened Redfish. Doused in tongue-tingling spices, the fish is cooked in a cast iron skillet heated over the highest heat to create a black crust on the outside and moist flesh on the inside. Some chefs maintain that the skillet can never be too hot for this dish. The version below maintains the sweet inner moistness, but you don't have to struggle with a red-hot skillet. A variety of pepper blends are available in the spice section of your supermarket—take your pick. Wallye sustitutes well for perch.

1/4 cup sweet paprika
1 1/2 teaspoons garlic powder
1 teaspoon Creole seasoning
1 teaspoon salt
4 (4- to 5-oz.) perch fillets, about
    1/2 inch thick
1/3 cup vegetable oil

① In resealable plastic bag, shake paprika, garlic powder, pepper blend and salt.

② Add perch fillets one at a time; shake to cover with spice mixture.

③ Heat oil in large skillet over medium-high heat until hot. Add fillets; cook 3 to 4 minutes per side or until dark brown, crusty and flaky in center.

④ Transfer to warm plates. Top each portion with chopped cilantro, parsley or a lime wedge.

4 servings.
Preparation time: 10 minutes.
Ready to serve: 20 minutes.

Per serving: 285 calories, 20 g fat (3 g saturated fat), 60 mg cholesterol, 760 mg sodium, 1.5 g fiber.

HOW TO FILLET FISH

In filleting fish, try to start the process by using a fillet knife that is as flexible as possible and has a narrow blade curving to a sharp point. It should also be razor sharp. See the photos below.

Lay the fish on a board; cut down to the spine and around the sides. Do not cut the spine in two. Cut into fish behind the transverse cut and slice toward the tail (1), cutting down to, but not through, the ribcage. When you have sliced down two-thirds of the length of the fish (where it begins to taper), push the knife point clear through (2), keeping the flat of the blade close along the backbone. Holding the fish with the left hand, continue to cut close against the backbone all the way to the tail. Now lay the fillet open and finish cutting the flesh away from the ribcage (3), slicing it loose along the belly line. Turn the fish over, and duplicate process on the other side.

To remove skin, place the fillet on the board, skin side down, and take hold of the tip of the fillet with the left hand. Cut in between skin and flesh, then change your grip with the left hand. Hold tight onto the skin tip while you slice forward (4), pressing the flat of the knife down as you slice forward.

FILLETING A FISH

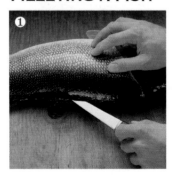

$\mathcal{M}$EAT

If you're a vegetarian, this isn't your chapter. But if you take delight in the juicy goodness of a nice cut of meat cooked in a way that really complements its natural flavor, then these recipes will make you very happy indeed.

MEAT

Heeding sensible dietary recommendations to eat in moderation, meat is once again back on American dinner tables. Today meat is leaner than ever before, thanks to carefully monitored feeding, breeding and processing methods.

Recipe cooking times are approximate. When meat is the subject, the tenderness of cuts varies, as does their fat content. Ovens, stoves, grills, particular pots and pans … these all make a difference too.

Use meat thermometers to determine temperature and doneness. When inserted, an instant-read thermometer will register within one minute. It is not designed to leave in the meat during cooking.

BEEF STEW

Cheaper cuts of meat—such as chuck or top round, which benefit by slow, moist cooking—make the best stews. Add a good, rich beef stock and/or wine, vegetables and herbs to enrich. The kitchen will be filled with appetizing aromas. If there are leftovers, they taste even better the next day. This recipe calls for a lot of vegetables for a healthy main dish. For speed and ease, use prepared baby carrots from the produce aisle and tiny onions from the freezer case.

1½	lb. beef chuck, cut into 1-inch pieces
2	tablespoons all-purpose flour
3	tablespoons vegetable oil
1	(¾-lb.) white turnip, cut into 1½-inch pieces
3	cups baby carrots
2	cups tiny onions
2	garlic cloves, halved
1	(14.5-oz.) can diced tomatoes
1	cup reduced-sodium beef broth
½	cup dry red wine
1	tablespoon Worcestershire sauce
⅛	teaspoon each salt, freshly ground pepper
1	cup fresh or frozen green beans, thawed
1	tablespoon unsalted butter

Buerre manie (French for kneaded butter), a smooth paste of equal quantities of butter and flour, is used to thicken soups, sauces and gravies. That is what you're creating in step 2. It is much less likely to lump than a paste of flour and water.

❶ Toss beef pieces in 1 tablespoon of the flour. Heat oil in Dutch oven or large saucepan over medium-high heat; brown meat on all sides. Stir in turnip, carrots and onions; toss 3 to 4 minutes until just brown. Add garlic, tomatoes, broth, wine, Worcestershire sauce, salt and pepper. Stir to combine.

❷ Reduce heat to a simmer. Cover and cook 2½ hours or until meat is tender. Add green beans. Cook an additional 3 to 5 minutes or just until beans have lost raw appearance. Blend remaining 1 tablespoon flour with butter.

❸ Push meat and vegetables to side of pot. To thicken gravy, drop tiny pieces of flour mixture into gravy, stirring constantly. Let simmer uncovered 5 minutes. Adjust seasoning, if desired.

4 to 6 servings.

Preparation time: 20 minutes.
Ready to serve: 3 hours.

Per serving: 570 calories, 33 g fat (11 g saturated fat), 115 mg cholesterol, 685 mg sodium, 7 g fiber.

BAKED GLAZED HAM

You'll use this recipe for many special occasions.

    1   (8- to 10-lb.) fully cooked smoked ham
    1/2 cup orange marmalade
    2   cups packed brown sugar
    2   tablespoons honey mustard
    1/2 cup whole cloves

1 Heat oven to 350°F. Place ham, fatty side up, on rack in large roasting pan.

2 Bake 2 hours or until internal temperature reaches at least 140°F. Set aside until cool enough to handle.

3 In small saucepan, heat marmalade over medium heat until hot and melted. In small bowl, combine sugar, mustard and marmalade. Set aside.

4 Remove peel and fat, leaving about 1/4-inch layer. With sharp knife, score diagonally through fat to make 1-inch diamonds.

5 Return meat to rack. Pat brown sugar mixture firmly into scored fat. Insert one whole clove into center of each diamond. Baste with any pan drippings.

6 Return to oven; bake an additional 20 minutes or until sugar mixture is melted and ham is glazed. Let rest 15 minutes before slicing. May be served at room temperature.

12 to 15 servings.

Preparation time: 10 minutes.
Ready to serve: 2 hours, 45 minutes.

Per serving: 745 calories, 38.5 g fat (12.5 g saturated fat), 155 mg cholesterol, 2415 mg sodium, 0.5 g fiber.

Almost all hams in the supermarket today are labeled fully cooked; however, that doesn't mean it should come to the table "au natural."

Roasting or braising in vegetables, juices, spices and wines tenderizes and permeates the meat with delicious flavors, and a glazed ham is the star of many a holiday table. Hams weigh in from 8 to 18 pounds, depending on the cut.

ROAST LEG OF LAMB

The classic way to roast a leg of lamb.

    1   (5- to 6-lb.) leg of lamb, trimmed
    4   garlic cloves, halved
    3   sprigs fresh rosemary or
            1 1/2 teaspoons dried
    2   teaspoons lemon-pepper seasoning
    1/2 lemon

1 Heat oven to 350°F. With sharp-pointed knife, cut 8 slits into lamb surface; insert one piece of garlic into each slit.

2 Place fatty side up on rack in large roasting pan. Rub with rosemary and lemon-pepper seasoning. Squeeze juice from lemon over meat, rubbing it in. Tuck lemon and rosemary on rack under meat.

3 Place in oven. Bake 1 1/4 hours or until internal temperature reaches at least 160°F. Let rest 20 minutes before serving.

8 to 10 servings.

Preparation time: 15 minutes.
Ready to serve: 1 hour, 45 minutes.

Per serving: 285 calories, 12.5 g fat (4.5 g saturated fat), 125 mg cholesterol, 185 mg sodium, 0 g fiber.

MEAT LOAF

A meat loaf should slice easily without crumbling, and taste equally delicious served hot or cold. Packages of meat loaf mixture—beef, pork and veal—are available in many markets, but use any combination you wish. If sausage meat is used, reduce the amount of salt and pepper you add.

1¹⁄₂	lb. lean ground beef
¹⁄₂	lb. ground turkey
¹⁄₄	lb. ground pork
¹⁄₂	cup finely chopped onion
1	scallion, thinly sliced
1	egg, beaten
¹⁄₂	cup fresh bread crumbs
¹⁄₄	cup reduced-sodium beef broth
³⁄₄	teaspoon salt
¹⁄₄	teaspoon freshly ground pepper
¹⁄₃	cup steak sauce

❶ Heat oven to 350°F. Spray 9x5-inch loaf pan with nonstick cooking spray.

❷ In large bowl, combine ground meats, onion, scallion, egg, bread crumbs, broth, salt, pepper and 2 tablespoons steak sauce; mix well. Shape mixture in pan.

❸ Pour remaining steak sauce over top, using knife or back of spoon to spread evenly.

❹ Bake 1¹⁄₄ to 1¹⁄₂ hours or until internal temperature reaches at least 160°F.

❺ Let rest 15 minutes before serving.

4 to 6 servings.
Preparation time: 20 minutes.
Ready to serve: 2 hours.

Per serving: 430 calories, 24 g fat (8.5 g saturated fat), 160 mg cholesterol, 1020 mg sodium, 1.5 g fiber.

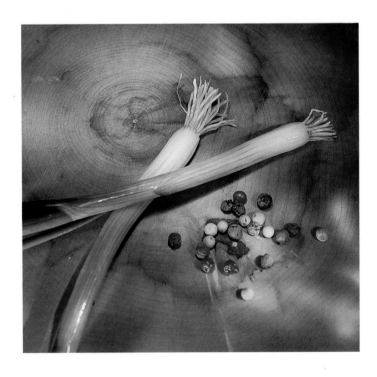

PORK CHOPS WITH DRIED-APPLE STUFFING

PORK CHOPS WITH DRIED-APPLE STUFFING

For this old-fashioned winter dish, choose chops 3/4 to 1 inch thick, so that a pocket can be cut in each. Usually the butcher will oblige, or you can do it yourself (see tip).

1/2	cup dried apples, cut into 1/2-inch pieces
1/2	cup apple cider or apple juice
3	tablespoons vegetable oil
3	large shallots, chopped
1/4	cup chopped celery
1	cup fresh brown bread crumbs
3/4	teaspoon dried sage
4	(8-oz.) center-cut pork chops
1/8	teaspoon each salt, freshly ground pepper
1/4	cup water

❶ Place apples in small bowl; pour cider over apples. Microwave on High power 1 1/2 minutes; drain and set aside, reserving liquid.

❷ In medium skillet, heat 2 tablespoons oil over medium-high heat until hot. Sauté shallots and celery until shallots begin to brown. Remove from heat. Add bread crumbs, sage, well-drained dried apples and just enough apple liquid to moisten; mix well.

❸ Heat broiler. Cut pocket in each pork chop*. Stuff mixture into pockets. Brush with remaining oil; sprinkle with salt and pepper. Arrange in 13x9-inch pan; place under broiler 1 to 2 minutes or until brown.

❹ Heat oven to 350°F. Secure stuffed pockets with toothpicks. Pour water into pan; cover tightly with aluminum foil. Bake 30 minutes. Uncover and bake an additional 20 minutes or until internal temperature reaches at least 160°F.

TIP *Make a pocket by using a sharp knife to cut towards the bone.

4 servings.
Preparation time: 15 minutes.
Ready to serve: 1 hour, 15 minutes.

Per serving: 550 calories, 30 g fat (8.5 g saturated fat), 100 mg cholesterol, 380 mg sodium, 2.5 g fiber.

TURKISH LAMB ROLL

Serve this aromatic meat roll with sour cream and cranberry sauce on the side.

1	tablespoon grated orange peel
1	tablespoon cinnamon
1 1/2	teaspoons ground cardamom
1 1/2	lb. lean ground lamb
1/4	cup water
1/2	cup chopped fresh dill
1 1/3	sheets frozen (thawed) puff pastry*
1	(8-oz.) can whole cranberry sauce or relish

❶ Heat oven to 375°F. Spray 9x5-inch loaf pan with nonstick cooking spray.

❷ In large cup, combine orange peel, cinnamon and cardamom.

❸ Place lamb, water and dill in large bowl. Sprinkle orange mixture over lamb. With clean hands, mix well to combine.

❹ Place 1 pastry sheet in loaf pan covering bottom, allowing edges to hang over sides. Spoon in lamb mixture; smooth with knife. Spread cranberry sauce or relish over. Bring up overhanging pastry sheet to cover. Pinch to seal. With sharp knife, make 4 (1/2-inch) cuts for steam to escape. Bake 1 hour. Let cool in pan 10 minutes.

TIP *Use remaining pastry from second sheet to cut out leaves to decorate. Mark with knife. Moisten lightly with a little water and press on lamb roll before baking.

6 to 8 servings.
Preparation time: 20 minutes.
Ready to serve: 1 hour, 30 minutes.

Per serving: 685 calories, 47.5 g fat (18 g saturated fat), 90 mg cholesterol, 225 mg sodium, 2.5 g fiber.

VEAL SCALOPPINE

Scaloppine are thin slices of meat, usually veal. To prepare, pound veal cutlets wafer-thin between sheets of parchment paper before cooking. If you don't have a wooden mallet, use the rounded end of a rolling pin. Clarified butter or a combination of butter and oil is used for frying to obtain buttery flavor. Butter alone should not be used at high frying temperatures, as the milk solids will scorch and become bitter-tasting. If desired, vegetable oil may be used, but you won't have the incomparable flavor that a bit of butter imparts.

1/3 cup all-purpose flour
1 teaspoon each dried oregano, lemon-pepper seasoning
1 egg, lightly beaten
1 1/2 cups fine fresh brown bread crumbs
8 slices veal cutlets, pounded (about 1 lb.)
2 tablespoons vegetable oil
2 teaspoons butter
1/2 cup white wine or reduced-sodium chicken broth
1/4 cup chopped mixed parsley and chives
2 tablespoons small capers, rinsed

❶ In large bowl, combine flour, oregano, and lemon-pepper seasoning; mix well. In medium bowl, beat egg at medium speed until frothy. In small bowl, measure out bread crumbs.

❷ Dredge veal cutlets in flour mixture to coat lightly. Dip in egg, then bread crumbs, pressing with fingers to help crumbs stick. Arrange cutlets on wire rack to dry. Refrigerate 20 to 30 minutes.

❸ Heat oven to 200°F. Heat oil and butter in large skillet over medium-high heat until hot and butter is melted. Sauté breaded cutlets 1 to 2 minutes per side until golden brown. Transfer cooked cutlets to warm ovenproof platter. Cover loosely with parchment paper. Keep warm in oven.

❹ Drain excess fat. Add white wine and 2 tablespoons parsley and chives to skillet. Stir to mix well. Bring to a boil over high heat; cook 3 to 4 minutes or until reduced slightly. Stir in capers.

Spoon sauce mixture over cutlets. Garnish with remaining herb mixture.

4 servings.
Preparation time: 45 minutes.
Ready to serve: 1 hour.

Per serving: 440 calories, 19.5 g fat (6 g saturated fat), 130 mg cholesterol, 635 mg sodium, 2 g fiber.

VARIATION **Cream Gravy with Shallots**
After removing cutlets from skillet, drain off any fat. Cook 3 chopped shallots over medium-high heat until softened and slightly browned. Stir in 1/2 cup whipping cream and 2 tablespoons chicken broth. Stir with wooden spoon. Simmer 3 to 4 minutes. Season with salt and pepper. Spoon over cutlets and serve.

Veal is the meat of a milk-fed young calf and should be pale pink in appearance. It is more tender and expensive than the more mature beef. Veal has little fat since it comes from a very young animal, usually eight to fifteen weeks old.

Scaloppine is the Italian word for "scallops." In our markets look for thin-sliced veal cutlets.

BEEF BRISKET WITH ROOT VEGETABLES

Here's a robust winter dinner dish that's easy to serve and tender enough to cut with a fork. It's perfect for a buffet or holiday table, dividing leftovers into family or single-size containers to freeze. Use a large disposable oven roasting bag for easy cleanup.

1 tablespoon all-purpose flour
1 (4-lb.) first cut brisket, trimmed
1 cup meatless marinara sauce
1/2 cup beer
3 bay leaves
3 medium onions, quartered
3 large carrots, cut into 1-inch pieces
2 large potatoes, cut into 1 1/2-inch pieces
1 large parsnip, sliced 1/2 inch thick
6 garlic cloves, halved
1/8 teaspoon salt
1/8 teaspoon freshly ground pepper

❶ Heat oven to 325°F. Dust inside of large roasting bag with flour; set in roasting pan. Place brisket in bag.

❷ In large bowl, combine marinara sauce, beer and bay leaves; mix well. Pour over meat, tilting bag to coat underside of meat.

❸ Arrange onions, carrots, potatoes, parsnip and garlic around meat, spooning some of the marinara mixture over vegetables.

❹ Tie bag closed. Cut 3 or 4 (1/2 inch) slits into bag.

❺ Cook 2 1/2 to 3 hours or until internal temperature reaches at least 160°F.

❻ Let rest 15 minutes before slicing. Discard bay leaves. Arrange sliced brisket and vegetables on warm platter.

❼ Skim fat from pan juices. Season with salt and pepper. Drizzle juices over brisket. Pour remainder into warm gravy boat and pass.

8 to 10 servings.

Preparation time: 25 minutes.
Ready to serve: 3 hours, 45 minutes.

Per serving: 655 calories, 43 g fat (17 g saturated fat), 135 mg cholesterol, 291 mg sodium, 4 g fiber.

SAUERBRATEN

For a special twist, use dried cherries instead of the traditional raisins. Ginger snaps are an instant thickener, melting into the gravy without any risk of lumping. The result is a lovely, rich, intensely sweet-and-sour sauce to go over the tender sliced meat. Allow at least 12 hours to marinate.

1¼ cups cider vinegar

1½ cups dry red wine

½ cup water

¾ cup packed brown sugar

1 teaspoon freshly ground pepper

1 teaspoon ground cloves

1 (3- to 4-lb.) boneless chuck, top round or brisket

¼ cup all-purpose flour

3 tablespoons vegetable oil

2 teaspoons minced garlic

3 scallions, cut into 2-inch pieces

¾ cup dried cherries

8 to 10 gingersnaps, crumbled

¼ cup sour cream

❶ In large saucepan, combine vinegar, wine, water, brown sugar, pepper and cloves. Bring to a boil over medium heat; remove from heat and cool.

❷ Place beef in 3-quart casserole. Pour marinade over beef, turning meat to coat. Cover tightly with plastic wrap; refrigerate at least 12 hours or overnight.Remove meat from marinade; pat dry with paper towels. Reserve marinade. Dredge meat in flour to coat.

❸ In Dutch oven or large pot, heat oil over medium-high heat until hot. Brown meat on all sides. Add 2½ cups of the marinade or enough to almost cover. Add garlic, scallions and cherries. Cover tightly and bring to a simmer. Reduce heat to low.

❹ Cook about 2½ hours or until meat is fork-tender. Transfer to carving board. Slice, cover and keep warm.Strain pan juices into pot. Gradually stir in enough gingersnaps to thicken gravy. Stir in sour cream; heat through. Pour some of the gravy over the sliced meat and serve.

6 to 8 servings.
Preparation time: 20 minutes.
Ready to serve: 14 hours.

Per serving: 618 calories, 38.5 g fat (14.5 g saturated fat), 105 mg cholesterol, 130 mg sodium, 1 g fiber.

If your pot isn't big enough to hold one large piece of meat, cut the piece in half across the grain and brown it, one piece at a time. Arrange both pieces in the pot, and add enough marinade to almost cover.

PASTA

It's hard to find a person who doesn't like pasta in one form or another. Unfortunately, pasta can also get a cook into a rut—making what he or she is good at and nothing else. Here's a range of recipe ideas, and plenty of variations, to keep things delicious and interesting.

PASTA

Say "pasta," and spaghetti and macaroni come to mind. But pasta is so much more. It's the generic Italian name for all dried starch products—of which there are more than 130 shapes and sizes depending on region. The popular belief is that Marco Polo probably brought a type of pasta from China to Italy, but versions of pasta-like dishes are found in ancient Roman recipes.

Pasta is basically a flour and water dough, with or without egg. The best pasta is made from hard durum wheat and cooks up tender but firm to the bite (al denté). Dry pasta, in dozens of varieties, is found on the supermarket shelves, in boxes or packages. Fresh pasta is available in the refrigerated or frozen section of the market, in gourmet stores or made at home with a pasta machine. Pastas are available tricolor and in trendy flavors such as spinach, tomato and whole wheat. In specialty shops you're likely to come across squid ink, chocolate and fruit flavors. Be adventurous and try them all. A fruit-flavored pasta could be used for Old City Noodle Pudding (page 103) and a tomato pasta would blend in with Pasta Primavera with Leafy Vegetables (page 106).

Pasta has become a firm favorite in American diets. It produces high-energy carbohydrates. It is low in fat. And, combined with meats, seafood and vegetables, pasta becomes a well-balanced meal. In addition, it's cheap, quick and easy to cook. A delicious one-dish meal can be prepared and on the table in minutes.

BUYING AND STORING PASTA

Dried Pasta—The most common is packaged in boxes. If there's a see-through window, check that the pasta's surface is smooth. Pasta with a mottled look may have been unevenly dried, and tends to fall apart during cooking.

Store pasta in a package or airtight container in a cool, dry place. Dried pasta may be stored up to 2 years, but for best quality and flavor, buy often and use as needed.

Fresh Pasta—Made with eggs, fresh pasta has a silky smooth texture. Pieces should be unbroken and dry, but not crumbly. Avoid packages that contain any moisture; pasta may be moldy and soft and mushy when cooked.

Fresh pasta is highly perishable and should be refrigerated. Use an unopened package by the expiration date marked. If only part of a package is used, wrap the remainder tightly in plastic wrap and use within 3 days. Exposed to the air, fresh pasta will quickly dry out and toughen.

Frozen Pasta—The pieces should be separate rather than frozen together. Packages should be airtight, undamaged and should not contain ice crystals or the dry, white spots that indicate freezer burn. Keep frozen until ready to cook.

Unopened pasta may be frozen in the original packaging up to 9 months but for best texture and flavor, use before 6 months.

PASTA COOKING TIPS

Here are some tips for cooking perfect pasta.

- Cook pasta according to package directions. To prevent sticking and clumping together, add pasta gradually to boiling water and stir occasionally during cooking. Use oil sparingly during cooking (about 1/2 teaspoon per pound). Too much oil will coat the pasta and prevent sauces from sticking after cooking.

- Check pasta for doneness at the minimum time. It should be cooked through and tender, but still firm and slightly chewy *(al dente)*.

- To serve cold, run cold water through pasta, drain thoroughly and toss with cooked vegetables or a zesty sauce.

- To reheat, place pasta in a colander and pour boiling water through, stirring gently. Drain and toss with a warm sauce; serve immediately.

- To microwave, cover loosely with parchment paper on Medium-High power 2 to 3 minutes for every 2 cups pasta. Stir once during cooking. Serve immediately.

- Approximately 4 ounces dry spaghetti yields 2 cups cooked. This varies according to the shape and type of pasta.

- For an appetizer or side dish serving, plan on 1/2 to 3/4 cup cooked pasta. For a main dish serving, allow about 1 1/2 cups cooked pasta.

MATCHING SHAPE AND SAUCE

The shapes of pastas serve a purpose. Combine pasta with sauce based on these traditional pairings:

- Pair fresh pastas, which are porous, with cream sauces, butter sauces and meat sauces. Do not pair fresh pastas with oil-based sauces.

- Use Capelli d'Angleo, the popular angel hair pasta, in soups and, perhaps, frittatas and soufflés. Sauces are too heavy for this pasta.

- Spaghettini is thinner than spaghetti and is excellent with light sauces such as pesto.

- Spaghetti is a good all-purpose noodle.

- Fusilli lunghi, also called fusilli col buco, is a long, coiled strand; it is perfectly suited to chunky sauces, such as ragu.

- Serve fettuccine with light cream-based sauces, such as Alfredo.

- Tagliatelle is twice as wide as fettuccine; its classic pairing is with Bolognese sauce.

- Papardelle is the widest noodle, and it can be paired with substantial sauces such as ragu, as well as butter-based sauces.

- Use seed-shaped pastas in soups, soufflés and frittatas, or sauce them very simply with butter and serve as a side dish.

- Pair tube-shaped pastas with ingredients of similar size; tube pastas work well with many olive-oil based sauces.

- Short strands, such as gemelli, al ceppo, casareccia and strozzapreti, are best paired with ingredients of similar length and width, such as julienned vegetables.

- Do not use instant lasagna noodles. They lack appealing texture.

HOMEMADE EGG NOODLES

In many areas, it's now possible to buy sheets of good quality, prepared pasta. If you're so inclined, you can make your own ravioli, tortellini or lasagna. But if you have a pasta machine, this recipe requires only the most basic of ingredients. The Swiss serve their hot cooked noodles in a simple manner—slathered in hot, melted butter and topped with crisp fried onions and grated sharp cheeses. Try it!

2	cups all-purpose flour
1/4	teaspoon salt
2	large eggs
1	tablespoon olive oil
2 to 3	tablespoons water

❶ In food processor, combine flour, salt, eggs, oil and enough water to process mixture into ball.

❷ Transfer mixture to bread board; knead 3 to 5 minutes or until smooth. Cover and let rest 10 minutes.

❸ Flatten dough with hands to width of pasta machine. Pass dough through several times until about 1/16 inch thick.

❹ Use cutting attachment on machine to cut into strands of desired width.

❺ Cook immediately, or if cooking within 24 hours, set aside on floured bread board covered with clean towel.

1 lb. pasta

Preparation time: 25 minutes.
Ready to serve: 30 minutes.

Per serving: 75 calories, 1.5 g fat (0.5 g saturated fat),
26.5 mg cholesterol, 44.5 mg sodium, 0.5 g fiber.

VARIATION **Mixed Herb Egg Noodles**
Add 2 teaspoons mixed dried herbs to flour before processing.

VARIATION **Whole Wheat Egg Noodles**
Substitute 1 cup whole wheat flour for 1 cup all-purpose flour.

VARIATION **Lemon and Poppy Seed Egg Noodles**
Add 2 teaspoons dried lemon peel and 2 teaspoons poppy seed to the flour mixture.

VARIATION **Pesto Pasta**
Reduce water to 1 tablespoon and add 2 tablespoons prepared pesto to the eggs, oil and water before mixing.

To make handcut pasta, roll 1/4 of the dough into a wafer-thin rectangle on a heavily floured board. Fold into thirds lengthwise. Cut crosswise into strips of desired width. Unfold and place on a lightly floured board. Dry about 1 hour at room temperature. (In some Italian villages, women still drape the noodles over a broom handle.)

LEMON AND POPPY SEED EGG NOODLES

COOKED TOMATO SAUCE

Capture the taste of summer with this sauce! Prepare sauce and pour into convenient containers or heavy plastic bags and freeze. If a thicker sauce is desired—with less cooking time—remove the seeds and juice from tomatoes before cooking.

1	Vidalia onion, cut into chunks
3	medium red ripe tomatoes, quartered
1/2	cup coarsely chopped fresh basil
1/4	cup parsley sprigs
2	teaspoons minced garlic
1/2	cup tomato sauce
	Dash crushed red pepper
2	teaspoons packed brown sugar
1/8	teaspoon salt

1 In food processor, finely chop onion, tomatoes, basil, parsley and garlic.

2 Transfer mixture to large pot. Add tomato sauce, red pepper and brown sugar; season with salt. Bring to a simmer over medium-high heat, stirring often. Reduce heat to low and cook, partially covered, 20 minutes or until thickened.

2 1/2 to 3 cups.
Preparation time: 15 minutes.
Ready to serve: 45 minutes.

Per serving: 55 calories, 0.5 g fat (0 g saturated fat), 0 mg cholesterol, 780 mg sodium, 2.5 g fiber.

VARIATION **Cooked Tomato Sauce with Mushrooms** Sauté 1/2 cup chopped mushrooms in 2 tablespoons oil; add to sauce before simmering.

VARIATION **Cooked Tomato Sauce with Apples** Add 1/4 cup unsweetened applesauce and 1/2 cup unpeeled chopped apple to mixture before simmering.

VARIATION **Barbeque-Flavored Cooked Tomato Sauce** Omit sugar and red pepper; replace canned tomato sauce with barbecue sauce.

VARIATION **Cooked Tomato Sauce with Olives** Add 1/2 cup chopped niçoise olives after 20 minutes simmer time. Season with salt at end of cooking time.

VARIATION **Cooked Tomato Sauce with Cream and Capers** Whisk in 1/4 cup sour cream and 3 tablespoons rinsed capers at end of cooking time.

VARIATION **Cooked Tomato Sauce with Chutney** Add 1/2 cup pureed chutney and 1/4 teaspoon curry powder at end of cooking time.

SPAETZLE

I first tasted these in a bierstube (bar-cafe) in Basel, Switzerland, and immediately became hooked on the tiny dumplings. I was even more amazed when I discovered how easy they are to make. They are a perfect foil for mild or pungent sauces and a sharp cheese, such as pecorino-Romano, made from sheep's milk (it is slightly granular with a bold, sharp flavor).

DUMPLINGS

1¼ cups all-purpose flour
1 teaspoon baking powder
½ teaspoon salt
2 eggs, lightly beaten
4 tablespoons butter, melted
¼ cup (1 oz.) freshly grated
    pecorino-Romano cheese
⅛ teaspoon freshly ground pepper

❶ In medium bowl, combine flour, baking powder and salt. Make well in center; gradually stir in eggs and 2 tablespoons of the butter, to make soft, workable dough. Cover with parchment paper or plastic wrap to prevent drying out. Let stand 30 minutes.

❷ In large pot, bring 1½ quarts water and 2 teaspoons salt to a boil.

❸ Shape mixture on floured board into long thin roll, about ½ inch thick.

❹ With kitchen scissors, snip ¼-inch pieces of dough into boiling water. Cook 3 to 4 minutes or until pieces rise to the surface; drain well.

❺ To serve, toss in remaining butter, grated cheese and pepper.

4 servings.
Preparation time: 45 minutes.
Ready to serve: 55 minutes.
Per serving: 530 calories, 19 g fat (10.5 g saturated fat), 150 mg cholesterol, 540 mg sodium, 2.5 g fiber.

> Spaetzle, "little sparrows" are extremely popular in southern Germany, Switzerland and Austria. Do not overcook or they will be tough. These freeze well before or after cooking. When preparing the dumplings, remember that the softer the dough, the lighter the dumplings will be.

FRESH CHUNKY TOMATO SAUCE

Ripe red tomatoes and green tomatoes combine in this uncooked sauce. Prepared in the food processor, there's no need to peel or seed the tomatoes. Use fresh basil, not dried. Add the sauce to fresh cooked pasta, spoon over poached fish or use to refresh leftover cooked vegetables.

4 medium red tomatoes, quartered
1 medium green tomato
2 scallions, cut into 2-inch pieces
2 tablespoons coarsely chopped fresh basil
1 teaspoon garlic powder
¼ cup vegetable juice
1 teaspoon Worcestershire sauce
⅛ teaspoon salt
⅛ teaspoon freshly ground pepper

❶ In food processor, coarsely chop tomatoes, scallions and basil.

❷ Transfer mixture to large bowl. Add garlic powder, vegetable juice and Worcestershire sauce.

❸ Stir to mix. Season with salt and pepper.

4 cups.
Preparation time: 15 minutes.
Ready to serve: 15 minutes.
Per serving: 50 calories, 1 g fat (0 g saturated fat), 0 mg cholesterol, 670 mg sodium, 2.5 g fiber.

VARIATION **Zesty Chunky Tomato Sauce**
Substitute zesty pizza or marinara sauce for the vegetable juice.

STUFFED MANICOTTI BAKED IN SALSA

Pancetta is a slightly salty, spiced Italian bacon that gives marvelous flavor to savory dishes such as pasta, sauces and vegetables. It comes in a tightly wrapped roll, and it may be refrigerated up to 3 weeks with no loss in flavor.

1	(1-lb.) jar mild salsa
3	large tomatoes, finely chopped
2	oz. pancetta, diced
2¼	cups part-skim ricotta cheese
1	cup (4 oz.) freshly grated Parmesan cheese*
1	egg, lightly beaten
2	tablespoons chives
	Dash freshly ground pepper
12	manicotti shells**

❶ Heat oven to 350°F.

❷ Spray 13x9-inch pan with nonstick cooking spray. In large bowl, mix salsa with tomatoes; set aside. In small saucepan, fry pancetta over high heat until crisp and brown. Remove from heat. Drain excess fat; cool. Add ricotta, ½ cup of the Parmesan, egg, chives and pepper; mix well. Using a teaspoon, stuff mixture into manicotti shells.

❸ Pour one-half of the salsa mixture into bottom of dish, spreading to cover bottom. Arrange manicotti over sauce in one layer. Cover with remaining salsa. Sprinkle with remaining Parmesan. Bake 1 hour or until sauce is bubbly and manicotti are tender.

TIP *Substitute ½ cup Manchego cheese for the Parmesan cheese filling. This is a rich, firm Spanish cheese. It will add a subtle, mellow flavor to this dish.

TIP **Manicotti does not have to be precooked, as the salsa-tomato mixture provides enough liquid to tenderize.

6 servings.

Preparation time: 30 minutes.
Ready to serve: 1 hour, 30 minutes.

Per serving: 325 calories, 11.5 g fat (6 g saturated fat), 65 mg cholesterol, 745 mg sodium, 3.5 g fiber.

PASTA PRIMAVERA WITH LEAFY VEGETABLES

Fresh or frozen vegetables may be used, but cook frozen vegetables first in microwave about 3 minutes on High power until barely tender. Squeeze out as much liquid as possible before adding to leeks in pan.

1/4	cup olive oil
2	leeks, cut into matchstick-size pieces
2	cups frozen baby broccoli florets, thawed
2	cups frozen cauliflower florets, thawed
6	Brussels sprouts
6	marinated artichoke hearts, quartered
1/4	cup sliced pitted ripe olives
2	tablespoons chopped pimiento
1	lb. spaghetti, drained
1/8	teaspoon garlic powder
1/8	teaspoon salt
1/8	teaspoon freshly ground pepper

❶ Heat olive oil in large skillet over medium heat. Sauté leeks until just brown. Increase heat to high. Stir in broccoli and cauliflower; cook until just lightly browned.

❷ Separate outer leaves from Brussels sprouts and shred remaining sprouts. Add to pan along with artichoke hearts. Heat thoroughly.

❸ Remove from heat; add olives and pimiento. Stir into hot, cooked spaghetti. Season with garlic powder, salt and pepper.

4 to 6 servings.

Preparation time: 25 minutes.
Ready to serve: 45 minutes.

Per serving: 370 calories, 17 g fat (2.5 g saturated fat), 0 mg cholesterol, 985 mg sodium, 9 g fiber.

MASTER

ROTINI WITH SORREL SAUCE

Sorrel, a sour green leafy herb, grows wild in Europe, Asia and parts of North America. It is available in spring, most often found in farmers' markets or specialty stores. Spinach may be substituted for all or part of the sorrel, adding a splash of cider vinegar to taste.

- 2 tablespoons olive oil
- 3 shallots, chopped
- 2 tablespoons all-purpose flour
- 4 cups shredded sorrel, packed
- 1/3 cup fresh dill, packed
- 1 small anchovy fillet, diced
- 1 cup reduced-sodium vegetable broth or water
- 1/2 cup half-and-half
- 1 lb. rotini, drained
- 1/3 cup shredded Parmesan or Romano cheese

❶ In medium saucepan, heat olive oil over medium heat until hot. Cook shallots 5 minutes or until softened. Stir in flour; reduce heat to medium-low and cook 1 minute, stirring constantly. Do not brown.

❷ Stir in sorrel and dill. When sorrel is bright green, add anchovy and broth. Bring to a simmer, stirring constantly.

❸ Reduce heat to low; cook 5 minutes. Add half-and-half; cool slightly. Puree mixture in food processor. Season with pepper. Pour mixture over hot cooked rotini; stir gently to mix. Sprinkle with cheese.

4 to 6 servings.
Preparation time: 25 minutes.
Ready to serve: 45 minutes.

Per serving: 610 calories, 15 g fat (5 g saturated fat), 18 mg cholesterol, 920 mg sodium, 6 g fiber.

MASTER

OLD-CITY NOODLE PUDDING

This peppery, sweet side dish remains a constant item on Jerusalem menus. When cooked, the pudding has a crisp, golden crust, so that it may be turned out onto a platter and cut in wedges. Any mixed dried fruits may be used. For a tropical twist, try chopped dried mango and pineapple, or chopped apples and prunes for the old fashioned taste of Eastern Europe.

- 1/2 cup vegetable oil
- 1/2 cup sugar
- 1 (8-oz.) pkg. vermicelli, cooked, drained
- 2 tablespoons grated orange peel
- 1 tablespoon freshly ground pepper
- 3/4 teaspoon salt
- 3 eggs, lightly beaten
- 1 1/2 cups chopped dried apricots
- 1/2 cup dried cherries

❶ Heat oven to 350°F. Spray 1 1/2-quart casserole with nonstick cooking spray.

❷ In medium saucepan, mix oil and sugar. Cook over medium heat, stirring constantly, until sugar turns golden, about 5 minutes.

❸ Remove from heat immediately. Stir in vermicelli, orange peel, pepper and salt. (If sugar becomes lumpy, return to low heat stirring until sugar melts. Cool slightly.)

❹ Add eggs, apricots and cherries; stir to mix.

❺ Transfer to casserole. Bake 50 to 60 minutes or until golden brown and firm when touched in center.

❻ Cool on wire rack 15 minutes. May serve from casserole or loosen sides with spatula and turn out onto platter. Serve warm or at room temperature.

6 to 8 servings.
Preparation time: 30 minutes.
Ready to serve: 1 hour, 30 minutes.

Per serving: 535 calories, 21.5 g fat (3.5 g saturated fat), 105 mg cholesterol, 480 mg sodium, 5 g fiber.

ENGLISH-STYLE LASAGNA

Inspired by a dish served to my assistant, Christine Galati, while she was visiting in London, this is a mouth-watering meal for everyone, including vegetarians. Prepared with oven-ready lasagna, which needs no precooking, two sheets fit nicely into a 8-inch square pan. A soy protein veggie ground round makes this dish quick, easy and impossible to distinguish from the traditional beefy version. And this one is much healthier for you.

1	cup Italian-flavored veggie ground round
2¼	cups marinara sauce
2	tablespoons butter
3½	tablespoons all-purpose flour
1	cup milk
1	cup (4 oz.) shredded Parmesan cheese
⅛	teaspoon each salt, freshly ground pepper, nutmeg
1	cup part-skim ricotta cheese
1	(10-oz.) pkg. frozen chopped spinach, thawed, squeezed dry
6	(2- to 3-oz.) sheets oven-ready lasagna noodles
1	teaspoon Italian seasoning

❶ Heat oven to 375°F. In large bowl, crumble veggie ground round into marinara sauce. Set aside.

❷ In small saucepan, melt butter over medium heat. Stir in flour; cook 1 minute, stirring constantly. Do not brown. Add milk; heat over high heat, whisking constantly. Cook an additional 1 minute. Remove from heat; stir in ½ cup of the Parmesan cheese. Season with salt, pepper and nutmeg. Set aside. In medium bowl, combine ricotta cheese and spinach. Set aside.

❸ To assemble, pour one-half of the marinara mixture over bottom of 13x9-inch pan. Place 2 sheets lasagna over sauce. Spread ricotta-spinach mixture over lasagna; cover with another 2 sheets lasagna. Pour over remaining marinara sauce; top with remaining 2 sheets lasagna. Cover with cheese sauce. Sprinkle with remaining ½ cup of the Parmesan cheese and Italian seasoning. Bake 25 to 30 minutes or until bubbly.

6 to 8 servings.

Preparation time: 35 minutes.
Ready to serve: 1 hour, 15 minutes.

Per serving: 545 calories, 19 g fat (9.5 g saturated fat), 45 mg cholesterol, 1045 mg sodium, 6 g fiber.

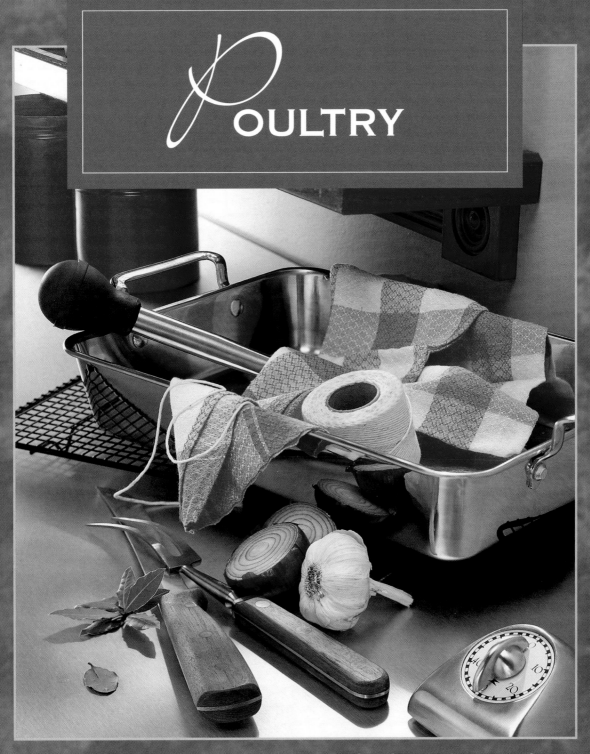

POULTRY

Poultry is affordable and, when cooked right, produces meals as wonderful as any other kind of meat. But as always, the recipes you use make the difference. Here are some essential classics you need, some great twists on old favorites, and some ideas that will be all new to your recipe repertoire too.

POULTRY

The term poultry covers all farmed fowl raised for meat and/or eggs. Classified by size, weight and age of the bird when processed, poultry includes chicken, capons, Cornish hens, turkey, duck, goose and squab. This meat is affordable, easy to cook and nutritionally low in fat and high in protein.

Poultry comes to the consumer ready to cook. There are no feathers to be plucked or chicken feet to be scraped as there was a couple generations ago. Supermarkets and butchers offer a wide selection, such as cut-up chicken and skinless and boneless breasts, as well as whole chickens. (See guide below.) Here is a guide to the other major classifications of poultry:

- *Turkeys, at one time only seen on holiday tables, are now available as light as 6 pounds, so that turkey can be cooked for the family throughout the year with few leftovers.*

- *Ducks weigh in at 4 to 6 pounds but contain a small proportion of rich meat to fat and bone. Most ducks that come to market are frozen and available year-round. Fresh ducks are available from late spring to early winter wherever ducks are farmed.*

- *Geese are not usually available in stores but must be specially ordered. Plan on 1 to 1½ pounds per serving. The most practical oven-ready fresh geese weigh between 7 and 11 pounds.*

- *Squabs, young pigeons, are farmed until they are about 4 weeks old. They weigh about 1 pound or less, and the meat is flavorful, tender and dark. Frozen squab is available year round.*

CHICKEN CLASSIFICATIONS

Each region and market has its own definitions and terminology for chickens. For example, broilers may be fried or grilled as well as broiled. Roasters may be braised or barbecued. All weights are ready-to-cook.

Broilers are young chickens, about 45 days old and weighing between 3¼ and 3½ pounds. An all-purpose chicken, they may be cooked by almost any method. Depending on where you live, broilers may be labeled as fryers.

Roasters are hens about 55 days old weighing and between 5 and 6 pounds.

Heavy Young Broiler Roasters are less than 10 weeks old and weigh between 6 and 8 pounds. They are sold fresh or frozen, both whole or cut up.

Stewing chickens are older birds, about 15 months old, no longer commercially productive for laying eggs. They weigh between 5 and 5½ pounds. They have exceptional flavor, but must be slow-cooked, as in a stock or stews.

The **Capon** is a castrated rooster, fed a fattening diet and brought to market between 14 and 15 weeks old. It weighs between 7 and 9 pounds. Full-breasted with a lot of white meat, the capon is best roasted.

There is much confusion about the terms free-range, hormone-free natural and organic chicken. Here's a guide:

Free-range: Realistically, the term "free-range" gives the impression that chickens are allowed to be in an outdoor area to forage for insects and other types of outdoor food. Because there is no official federal government definition, the U.S. Department of Agriculture (U.S.D.A.) approves label claims on a case-by-case basis, generally if access to the outside is available for at least part of the day.

Hormone-free: No artificial or added hormones or steroids are allowed by the U.S. government in the production of chickens in this country. According to the National Chicken Council, any brand could be advertised hormone-free.

Natural: Under U.S.D.A. regulations, a "natural" product has no added ingredients and is minimally processed, just enough to get it ready to be cooked.

Organic: The concept of organic production generally prohibits the use of artificial pesticides and manufactured fertilizers. Organically produced chickens must be fed a diet of organically produced feeds.

BUYING POULTRY

New chicken and poultry cuts are appearing daily in the supermarkets and farmers' markets. Choose carefully. Here are some guidelines for the best quality:

- Packages should be in the refrigerated section, and be cold to the touch.
- Check sell-by date on the label. Though this notes the last day the poultry should be sold, it may be safely cooked and eaten within two days after the date.
- Packages should not be damaged and poultry should not be discolored (bruised or bloody). The skin should be clean and smooth and the meat plump and moist. Skin color depends on the poultry feed and may range from pearly white to pale yellow. Color does not indicate any difference in nutritional value, flavor or tenderness.
- If poultry smells when the package is opened, get your money back. All poultry should smell fresh without foul odors.
- Each package of fresh poultry carries a U.S.D.A.-mandated safe food message. Follow it carefully.

- Before and after preparing any poultry, hands and utensils must be scrupulously cleaned. Wash countertops, cutting boards, knives and other utensils in hot soapy water, then rinse in cold water.
- When barbecuing, keep poultry refrigerated until ready to cook. Serve on a clean dish. Do not place cooked poultry on the same plate used to carry raw meat to the grill.
- Shop for perishables, such as chicken, last. And refrigerate immediately on getting home. Never leave poultry in a hot car or on a countertop at room temperature.

STORING POULTRY

Chicken and other poultry is highly perishable and should be handled with care.

- **To store** packaged fresh poultry, refrigerate in original wrapping in coldest part of refrigerator 1 to 2 days.
- **To freeze** uncooked poultry, use large resealable plastic bags. Squeeze as much air as possible out of bags before sealing. Label and date.
- **To thaw**, place poultry in refrigerator, not on countertop or in cold water. It takes approximately 24 hours to thaw a 4-lb. chicken in the refrigerator; cut-up parts take 3 to 9 hours depending on quantity and size.

- **Cooked**, cut-up chicken (or other poultry) is at its best when refrigerated no longer than two days. After that it tends to dry out, even when tightly wrapped. Cooked whole chicken may be refrigerated an additional day.
- If chicken or poultry is **stuffed**, remove the stuffing and store that in a separate container before refrigerating or freezing.
- Do not refreeze cooked or uncooked poultry once it has been thawed.

ROAST CHICKEN

Roasting breast side down during the first 30 minutes of cooking time will help keep the meat juicy and flavorful, but basting is essential for a moist, tender chicken. Baste often (about every 15 minutes) using oil, butter, stock or pan drippings. Before cooking be sure to remove the giblets (the neck, liver, heart and gizzard), which are usually in a package in the chicken's cavity. Plan on approximately 1/2 cup stuffing per pound of poultry.

1 (3½-lb.) broiler-fryer chicken

⅛ teaspoon salt

⅛ teaspoon freshly ground pepper

2 garlic cloves, halved

½ lemon, cut into 2 or 3 pieces

1 sprig rosemary or thyme

2 tablespoons vegetable oil

❶ Heat oven to 375°F.

❷ Remove excess fat and giblets; set giblets aside. Wash chicken and pat dry. Season inside cavity with salt and pepper. Tuck in garlic, lemon and rosemary. Secure drumsticks with string.

❸ Place chicken breast side down, on rack set in baking pan; brush with oil. Bake 30 minutes, basting once or twice with pan juices.

❹ Turn chicken breast side up. Reduce heat to 350°F. Continue baking, basting often, an additional 45 minutes to 1 hour or until internal temperature reaches 180°F. Let stand at room temperature 10 to 15 minutes before carving.

4 servings.

Preparation time: 15 minutes.
Ready to serve: 2 hours.

Per serving: 445 calories, 27 g fat (7 g saturated fat), 145 mg cholesterol, 710 mg sodium, 0 g fiber.

VARIATION **Simple Crouton Stuffing**
Omit garlic and lemon from Roast Chicken. To make the stuffing, sauté 1 chopped small onion and 1 rib chopped celery in ¼ cup margarine. Remove from heat; fold in 2 cups seasoned croutons, ¼ teaspoon ground thyme and about 3 tablespoons reduced-sodium chicken broth (enough to moisten stuffing). If you don't have chicken broth, mix 3 tablespoons water with 1 teaspoon Worcestershire sauce. Stuff loosely into cavity. Secure drumsticks with string. Bake as directed for *Roast Chicken* until internal temperature reaches at least 180°F.

ROAST TURKEY

If the turkey is frozen, here's how to thaw it properly (see chart). Turkey must be cooked very soon after thawing. Stuff the turkey just before roasting and do not refrigerate a stuffed turkey. All utensils and hands must be thoroughly clean before handling to prevent the growth of harmful bacteria, including salmonella.

1 (10- to 12-lb.) turkey
1/8 teaspoon salt
1/8 teaspoon freshly ground pepper
2 tablespoons butter
2 onions, quartered*
2 tablespoons vegetable oil

❶ Heat oven to 325°F.

❷ Remove giblets from cavity; set giblets aside for stock or gravy. Wash turkey and pat dry.

❸ Season cavity with salt and pepper. Add butter and onions, spreading around with fingers. Secure drumsticks with string. Generously rub vegetable oil over skin.

❹ Place turkey, breast side up, on rack in large roasting pan. Bake, basting every 30 minutes, 3½ to 4 hours, or until internal temperature reaches 180°F**.

❺ Let rest 30 minutes before carving to allow juices to be absorbed back into meat.

TIP *Omit onions if stuffing turkey.

TIP **If turkey browns too quickly, place tent of aluminum foil loosely over.

13 servings.
Preparation time: 20 minutes.
Ready to serve: 4 hours, 30 minutes.

Per serving: 185 calories, 4.5 g fat (1.5 g saturated fat), 85 mg cholesterol, 265 mg sodium, 0 g fiber.

VARIATION **Giblet Stuffing**
Chop cooked giblets finely (See *Turkey Stock*) for cooking giblets). In large bowl, add 3½ cups cooked, seasoned rice, 1 cup chopped Vidalia onion, 1 cup diced mushrooms, ½ cup chopped fresh parsley, ¼ cup chopped fresh tarragon, 3 tablespoons melted margarine and salt and pepper to giblets. Fill turkey cavity loosely with stuffing; bake.

VARIATION **Currant and Cornbread Stuffing**
In large skillet over medium heat, sauté 2 medium chopped onions and 2 ribs thinly sliced celery in 3 tablespoons margarine or butter until soft. Remove from heat; add 4 cups slightly dry, crumbled cornbread, ¾ cup dried currants, 2 tablespoons grated orange peel, 1 beaten egg and ½ cup chopped fresh parsley. If needed, add 2 to 3 tablespoons water or reduced-sodium chicken broth to moisten. Season with salt and pepper. Stuff mixture loosely into turkey cavity. Any extra stuffing may be baked in separate buttered baking dish at 350°F. Keep moist by basting with a little broth and loosely cover with aluminum foil. Bake turkey.

VARIATION **Sausage, Apple and Couscous Stuffing** Prepare 1 (5.8-oz.) pkg. Roasted Garlic and Olive Oil Couscous according to package directions. Set aside. Crumble 1-lb. well-seasoned sausage meat into large saucepan. Cook over medium heat 5 minutes, stirring often. Add 2 chopped Granny Smith apples; cook an additional 5 minutes or until internal temperature reaches at least 160°F. Stir in 2½ cups cooked couscous, ½ cup chopped fresh parsley, 2 tablespoons chopped fresh cilantro and 2 teaspoons fines herbes. Season with salt and pepper. Stuff mixture loosely into cavity; truss and bake.

VARIATION Simple Turkey Gravy

Remove most of fat from roasting pan leaving about 3 tablespoons. Whisk in 3 tablespoons all-purpose flour; cook over medium heat 1 minute, stirring constantly. Add 1¾ cups reduced-sodium chicken broth or water. Bring to a boil, stirring and scraping brown bits from bottom of pan. Stir until thickened. Whisk in 2 tablespoons dry white wine. Season with salt and pepper.

VARIATION Cream Gravy

Whisk in 2 tablespoons sour cream instead of white wine.

VARIATION Mushroom Gravy

Substitute red wine for white wine. Stir in ½ cup sliced sautéed mushrooms.

VARIATION Onion Gravy

Sauté 1 small, finely chopped onion in fat before adding flour and reduced-sodium chicken broth. Stir in 2 tablespoons chopped fresh parsley.

VARIATION Turkey Stock

Place giblets (gizzard, liver and heart) in large saucepan with water to cover. Add 3 parsley sprigs, 1 sliced celery rib and 1 teaspoon salt. Cover and cook 1 hour, adding more water, if needed. Cool. Chop giblets coarsely and add to turkey gravy or to enhance a store-bought stuffing mix.

Many turkeys come with a pop-up thermometer. But when using that thermometer, much of the time the meat becomes overcooked and dry.

The most accurate way to tell if the turkey is done is to use an instant-read thermometer inserted in the thickest part of the breast. For turkey, bake until internal temperature reaches 180°F.

Trussing helps make the bird look plump and keeps the meat and stuffing from drying out. It involves securing the legs and wings close to the turkey's body with string or poultry skewers, which are available in hardware and kitchen stores. At Thanksgiving, you may even find them in your market above the poultry. If you use a V-shaped rack, trussing may not be necessary because the legs and wings are pressed against the turkey body, plumping up the breast.

BASIC TURKEY GRILLING TIMES AND TECHNIQUES

In case you want to grill a turkey, here are some guidelines.

Type	Weight	Grilling Method	Fire Method	Doneness Temperature	Cook Time
Whole	9-15 lbs.	Indirect	Hot/ banked	180°F	15 min./lb.
Halved	10-12 lbs.	Indirect	Hot/ banked	180°F	1½-2 hrs.
Breast halves with bone	10-12 lbs.	Indirect	Hot/ banked	180°F	1-1½ hrs.
Drumsticks/ thighs	1-2 lbs. each	Direct covered	Medium	No pink meat near bone	55-65 min.
Boneless cubes	1 inch	Direct	Medium	No pink meat when cut	12-15 min.
Breast steaks	½-inch thick	Direct	Medium	No pink meat when cut	7-9 min.

CRISPY ROAST DUCK

Duck tends to be very fatty and a bit tricky to cook. Start off at a high temperature and baste often during cooking to help crisp the skin. Use a large roasting pan so that halfway through cooking, the duck can be turned and the fat poured off.

DUCK

1	(4- to 5-lb.) duck
2	bay leaves
1	onion, quartered
1	orange, sliced
1/8	teaspoon salt
1/8	teaspoon freshly ground pepper

SOUR CHERRY SAUCE

2	tablespoons packed brown sugar
1/2	cup dry red wine
1	tablespoon cornstarch
1	(15-oz.) can pitted sour cherries, drained, juice reserved
	Dash nutmeg

❶ Heat oven to 475°F. Set oven rack in large roasting pan.

❷ Remove giblets; set aside or freeze to make stock at another time. Trim wing tips from duck. Remove excess fat; wash duck and pat dry.

❸ Tuck bay leaves, onion and orange in cavity; season with salt and pepper. Prick breast all over; season skin with additional salt and pepper, if desired.

❹ Place duck on rack, breast side down. Bake 30 minutes, basting every 15 minutes with pan juices. Reduce oven temperature to 375°F.

❺ Carefully remove roasting pan from oven; place duck on cutting board. Very carefully remove most of the fat from pan, leaving enough to baste. Return duck to rack, breast side up.

❻ Continue baking an additional 1½ hours, basting occasionally, until skin is brown and crispy and internal temperature reaches 180°F.

❼ Drain off excess fat from roasting pan. Add brown sugar and wine; stir frequently. Cook over high heat until one-half of the wine has evaporated. Reduce heat to medium.

❽ In small bowl, blend cornstarch and 1/4 cup cherry juice at high speed until smooth; set aside. Add remaining juice, cherries and nutmeg to pan; bring to a boil. Add cornstarch mixture, stirring constantly until thickened and clear.

❾ Transfer duck to serving platter. Let rest 10 minutes before cutting with shears into halves or quarters. Spoon Sour Cherry Sauce over duck; serve hot.

2 to 4 servings.

Preparation time: 15 minutes.
Ready to serve: 2 hours, 30 minutes.

Per serving: 1490 calories, 109 g fat (37 g saturated fat), 320 mg cholesterol, 235 mg sodium, 3 g fiber.

COQ AU VIN

Coq au Vin, chicken cooked in wine, is one of the oldest recipes in French country cooking. Influenced by the grand dame of cuisine, Julia Child, the dish became popular with Americans in the 1950's and is still a firm favorite. Coq au Vin may be simmered on the stovetop or baked in a casserole at 350°F.

1   (3½-lb.) fryer-broiler chicken, cut into
     8 pieces
½   cup all-purpose flour
1   teaspoon poultry seasoning
2   tablespoons butter
2   tablespoons olive oil
3   tablespoons warm cognac
1   cup dry red wine
⅓   cup reduced-sodium chicken broth
1   (2-oz.) slice cooked ham, chopped
1   cup fresh or frozen baby onions, thawed
8   medium mushrooms, halved
2   teaspoons chopped garlic
½   teaspoon dried thyme
2   bay leaves
⅛   teaspoon salt
⅛   teaspoon freshly ground pepper
1   tablespoon chopped fresh parsley

❶ Wash chicken and pat dry. In resealable plastic bag, combine flour and poultry seasoning; toss chicken pieces in flour mixture to coat.

❷ Heat butter and oil in large skillet over medium heat. Add chicken pieces; cook until golden brown on all sides and no longer pink in center.

❸ Remove skillet from heat. Pour cognac over chicken; ignite with long taper or match. When flame has died down, add wine, broth, ham, onions, mushrooms, garlic, thyme, and bay leaves. Season with salt and pepper; stir gently to mix.

❹ Cover tightly and simmer over low heat 1½ hours or until chicken is tender and internal temperature reaches 180°F. Remove bay leaves. Garnish with chopped parsley.

4 servings.
Preparation time: 25 minutes.
Ready to serve: 2 hours, 15 minutes.

Per serving: 610 calories, 34.5 g fat (11 g saturated fat), 170 mg cholesterol, 1055 mg sodium, 1.5 g fiber.

ROCK CORNISH HENS ROASTED WITH PEPPER

Rock Cornish game hens are a cross between a Cornish game cock and a White Plymouth Rock chicken. These miniature chickens are 4 to 6 weeks old and are all white meat. They may weigh up to 2$\frac{1}{2}$ pounds, although 1$\frac{1}{2}$ pounds or less is more usual. That's enough for one serving. Larger birds may be halved to make two servings. Roasting is the easiest and best cooking method for whole Rock Cornish hens. If desired, 1 tablespoon well-rinsed small capers mixed with $\frac{1}{2}$ teaspoon packed brown sugar may be substituted for pink peppercorns. A black and white peppercorn mixture is available in the spice section of the market.

4 (1$\frac{1}{2}$-lb.) Rock Cornish game hens

$\frac{1}{8}$ teaspoon kosher (coarse) salt

1 tablespoon plus 1 teaspoon freshly ground pepper

1 tablespoon plus 1 teaspoon freshly ground white pepper

1 tablespoon chopped pink peppercorns

2 large scallions, cut into 4 pieces

1 mild yellow chile, seeded, quartered

2 ribs celery, cut into 4 pieces

$\frac{1}{4}$ cup unsalted butter, melted

❶ Heat oven to 450°F. Line 15x10x1-inch baking sheet with aluminum foil. Wash hens and pat dry. Season cavities with salt and peppers.

❷ In each cavity, sprinkle $\frac{3}{4}$ teaspoon pink peppercorns; stuff with 2 pieces scallion, $\frac{1}{4}$ of the chile pepper and 2 pieces of the celery. Secure drumsticks with string. Arrange on baking sheet, breast side up.

❸ In large cup, combine melted butter with 1 tablespoon plus 1 teaspoon each of black and white pepper.

❹ Brush Cornish hens generously with mixture. Bake 10 minutes. Reduce heat to 350°F. Turn hens onto sides, baste with butter mixture. Bake 10 minutes per side. Return hens to breast side up, baste again with butter mixture and continue baking an additional 30 minutes or until internal temperature reaches 180°F.

4 servings.
Preparation time: 25 minutes.
Ready to serve: 1 hour, 30 minutes.

Per serving: 710 calories, 53.5 g fat (19 g saturated fat), 330 mg cholesterol, 750 mg sodium, 1 g fiber.

Pink peppercorns are the dried berries from a rose plant cultivated in Madagascar. They are not a true peppercorn. They have a slightly sweet flavor and are available in gourmet stores, freeze-dried or packed in brine. They are used for aesthetic appearance, color and flavor in meat, fish and poultry dishes, as well as sauces.

CHICKEN BREASTS WITH APRICOT-PISTACHIO STUFFING

Pretzels form the base of this bold stuffing. Bake separately in a baking dish or well-greased individual muffin pans. Or tuck pretzel stuffing under the chicken breasts. The stuffing may be made in advance and refrigerated, but to avoid contamination, do not place under chicken until just before cooking. The classic mixture of fines herbes *includes chervil, chives, parsley and tarragon and is available in the market.*

STUFFING

- 1½ cups crushed pretzels
- 2 ribs celery, cut into 2-inch pieces
- 10 dried apricot halves
- ¼ cup shelled pistachios
- 1½ teaspoons dried fines herbes
- ¼ cup plus 4 teaspoons margarine, melted
- 2 tablespoons water

CHICKEN

- 4 (8-oz.) chicken breasts
  Dash paprika

❶ Heat oven to 350°F.

❷ Spray 8-inch square pan with nonstick cooking spray.

❸ In food processor, chop pretzels, celery, apricots and pistachios until coarse bread crumbs form. Add fines herbes, 3 tablespoons of the margarine and water; process to mix.

❹ Place ¼ cup of the mixture into pan. Arrange one chicken breast on top; press lightly. Repeat with remaining stuffing and chicken breasts. Bake any extra stuffing separately.

❺ Slip 1 teaspoon of the margarine under skin of each chicken breast. Brush chicken with remaining margarine. Sprinkle lightly with paprika.

❻ Bake 1 hour or until internal temperature reaches 180°F.

4 servings.
Preparation time: 25 minutes.
Ready to serve: 1 hour, 30 minutes.

Per serving: 540 calories, 31.5 g fat (6 g saturated fat), 97 mg cholesterol, 565 mg sodium, 3.5 g fiber.

> For individual servings, fill 4 to 6 well-greased mini soufflé dishes about ¾ full. Drizzle with a little oil or melted margarine and bake the last 15 to 20 minutes of cooking time until nicely browned. Or spoon into a well greased 1-quart dish and bake at 350°F for 30 minutes or until crusty on top.

TURKEY DIVAN

This is an updated and lightened version of the old classic. Nondairy creamer or half-and-half is used instead of heavy whipping cream, and sliced water chestnuts are added to timesaving frozen, cooked broccoli florets. The result is a dish elegant enough for company, but it can also be quickly assembled for the family. Turkey Divan is a great way to use up leftover turkey. But fully cooked, roasted turkey breast or cooked boneless chicken may be purchased at the market and used here.

1	(14-oz.) bag frozen baby broccoli florets, thawed
1	cup sliced water chestnuts
1/4	cup each margarine, all-purpose flour
1 1/2	cups reduced-sodium chicken broth
1/4	cup half-and-half
3	tablespoons sherry or vermouth
1	teaspoon Worcestershire sauce
	Dash nutmeg
1 1/4	cups (5 oz.) freshly grated Parmesan cheese
3/4	lb. cooked sliced turkey
	Dash paprika

❶ Heat oven to 425°F.

❷ Cook broccoli florets in microwave 6 to 7 minutes on High power; drain well. Transfer to 3-quart casserole. Scatter water chestnuts over broccoli; set aside.

❸ In medium saucepan, melt margarine over medium heat; add flour. Let mixture cook while stirring briskly 1 minute.

❹ Add broth, whisking constantly until mixture comes to a boil. Cook an additional 1 to 2 minutes or until thickened. Remove from heat. Add half-and-half, sherry, Worcestershire sauce, nutmeg and 3/4 cup of the Parmesan cheese. Stir well until smooth.

❺ Arrange sliced turkey over vegetables. Pour sauce over vegetables, spreading with spoon to cover. Sprinkle with remaining Parmesan cheese and paprika. Bake 20 to 30 minutes or until internal temperature reaches 180°F and topping is hot and bubbly.

6 servings.

Preparation time: 15 minutes.
Ready to serve: 1 hour, 15 minutes.

Per serving: 340 calories, 19 g fat (7 g saturated fat), 65 mg cholesterol, 825 mg sodium, 2.5 g fiber.

CONFETTI FLANNEL HASH

Keep this dish refrigerated before baking. Before refrigerating, cover the surface with parchment paper or plastic wrap to prevent drying.

3/4 lb. cooked turkey, cut into 2-inch pieces

1/4 cup vegetable oil

2 small leeks, sliced (white and green parts)

1 red bell pepper, cored, seeded, diced

1 cup cooked rice*

1/2 teaspoon dried sage

1/8 teaspoon salt

1/8 teaspoon freshly ground pepper

❶ Heat oven to 375°F. Spray 1½-quart casserole with nonstick cooking spray.

❷ In food processor, pulse turkey into ¾-inch pieces; set aside.

❸ In medium saucepan, heat 3 tablespoons oil over medium-high heat. Fry leeks and bell pepper until just brown.

❹ Reduce heat to medium. Stir in turkey, rice and dried sage. Season with salt and pepper. Stir constantly until heated through.

❺ Transfer to casserole. Drizzle with remaining oil. Bake 20 minutes or until heated through and golden brown.

TIP *About ⅓ cup raw white, long grain rice yields 1 cup cooked.

4 to 6 servings.
Preparation time: 20 minutes.
Ready to serve: 1 hour.

Per serving: 345 calories, 19 g fat (3.5 g saturated fat), 70 mg cholesterol, 805 mg sodium, 1.5 g fiber.

HUNTER'S STEW

Originally this stew was prepared with rabbit, pheasant or other gamebird, venison or whatever the hunter brought home. Quick-cooking chicken and Polish sausage are used here, but tough cuts of meat, such as cubed venison shoulder or beef shanks, are flavorful and tender when cooked using this method.

CHICKEN

  1/4 cup all-purpose flour
   2   teaspoons poultry seasoning
  1/2 teaspoon sweet paprika
 1 1/2 lb. chicken drumsticks and thighs
  1/4 cup vegetable oil
   2   cups frozen mixed stewing vegetables, thawed
  1/2 cup fresh or frozen corn kernels, thawed
  1/2 lb. kielbasa, sliced (1/2 inch thick)
   1   (14.5-oz.) can diced tomatoes with basil
  1/4 cup water

DUMPLINGS

   1   cup all-purpose flour
 1 1/2 teaspoons baking powder
  1/2 teaspoon salt
   1   tablespoon margarine, chilled
 1 1/2 tablespoons vinaigrette dressing
  1/2 cup skim milk

❶ In resealable plastic bag, combine flour, poultry seasoning and paprika. Add chicken pieces; seal bag. Toss to coat with flour mixture. Set aside.

❷ Heat oil in large saucepan over medium heat. Add chicken pieces; cook 8 to 10 minutes until golden brown on all sides and no longer pink in center.

❸ Add stewing vegetables, corn, kielbasa, tomatoes and water; stir gently to mix. Reduce heat to a simmer; cover and cook 50 minutes.

❹ About 20 minutes before end of cooking time, prepare dumplings. In large bowl, combine flour, baking powder and salt. Cut in margarine with pastry blender or fingers until mixture crumbles. Make well in center; add dressing and enough milk to form soft dough.

❺ Drop dumpling mixture by heaping tablespoons into hot stew, taking care not to drop directly into gravy. Simmer, uncovered, 10 minutes. Simmer, covered, an additional 10 minutes or until dumplings are dry and fluffy inside.

4 to 6 servings.

Preparation time: 25 minutes.
Ready to serve: 1 hour, 30 minutes.

Per serving: 850 calories, 54 g fat (13 g saturated fat), 112 mg cholesterol, 1230 mg sodium, 7.5 g fiber.

SALADS

Salads need not be hum-drum. They can be fantastic! With these ideas—for dressings you can make (incomparably better than store-bought), green salads and some creations beyond—salad will become a high-point of any meal and not an obligation.

$\mathcal{S}$ALADS

$\mathcal{T}$hink salads? Think greens! Green leafy salads have never been easier. Today, every supermarket carries an incredible variety of greens ... from iceberg lettuce, the darling of the 1950's, to trendy favorites such as radicchio, oak-leaf lettuce, arugula and mesclun (a mixture of baby greens). They may be purchased in bags, already washed and 100% ready to use —a boon to today's busy lifestyles.

In this chapter, besides a variety of salads, you'll find essentials such as coleslaw, Caesar and egg salad, along with accompanying essential dressings.

TO BUY, WASH AND STORE SALAD GREENS

To Buy: Choose loose leaves that are crisp and fresh. Ignore any produce that is wilted, droopy and discolored.

To Wash: Wash in cold, slightly salted water, swishing around to dislodge any sediment or sand. A salad spinner is a worthwhile investment. Spinning leaves in a salad spinner will remove the water so that leaves are almost dry. Wet leaves will dilute the dressings, and if stored, even for one day or so, they will wilt and become slimy.

To Store Greens: Line resealable plastic bag with paper towels. Add dried greens and top with another paper towel before sealing. Refrigerate. Cleaned and packaged like this, greens will keep fresh for up to three days.

To Store Leafy Herbs: Swish herbs in several changes of cold water until the water remains clean. Shake dry or spin in a salad spinner. Place in paper towel-lined resealable plastic bag and refrigerate. Herbs will stay fresh up to 5 days. Before chopping, make sure herbs are completely dry, or they will lump together and become impossible to sprinkle.

COOKED MAYONNAISE

If you're hesitant about using raw egg yolks, as in the traditional mayonnaise recipe, use this cooked method based on a recipe from the American Egg Board. It produces a rich, creamy mayonnaise. The oil should be added in a very slow, steady stream. If added too quickly, the mixture may curdle, separate or never thicken. Ingredients should be at or close to room temperature before starting. See the variations listed to turn this building block ingredient into great dressings!

2 egg yolks
2 tablespoons cider vinegar or fresh lemon juice
2 tablespoons cold water
3/4 teaspoon sugar
1 teaspoon dry mustard
1/2 teaspoon salt
    Dash cayenne pepper
1 cup peanut or vegetable oil

❶ In small saucepan, whisk egg yolks, vinegar and water. Cook over low heat, stirring constantly, until mixture just begins to thicken.

❷ Remove from heat. Place saucepan over bowl of ice water 1 minute to stop cooking; scrape mixture into blender. Add sugar, mustard, salt and cayenne. Blend 1 or 2 seconds at medium speed. Let stand at room temperature 5 minutes.

❸ With blender running, cover and drizzle in a few drops of oil. Continue to add oil in slow, steady stream; blend until thick and smooth. Pour into clean container. Cover and refrigerate.

1 1/3 cups.

Preparation time: 5 minutes.
Ready to serve: 35 minutes.

Per serving: 105 calories, 11.5 g fat (2 g saturated fat), 20 mg cholesterol, 60 mg sodium, 0 g fiber.

VARIATION Tartar Sauce
Stir in 3 tablespoons chopped pickle and 1 teaspoon chopped chives to 1 cup mayonnaise.

VARIATION Russian Dressing
Stir in 1/2 cup chili sauce to 1 cup mayonnaise.

VARIATION Thousand Island Dressing
Add 2 tablespoons milk, 2 tablespoons ketchup, 2 tablespoons pickle relish, 2 teaspoons chopped pimento, 1 chopped, hard-cooked egg and 1/2 teaspoon sweet paprika to 1 cup mayonnaise. Season with salt and ground white pepper.

VARIATION Blue Cheese and Chive Dressing
Stir 1/4 cup crumbled blue cheese and 2 tablespoons finely chopped chives into 1 cup mayonnaise.

In mayonnaise, egg yolk is the emulsifying agent binding oil and vinegar or lemon juice. The egg yolk contains natural emulsifiers, which coat liquids with fats, thus creating a smooth, creamy texture. It also provides color, flavor and nutrients.

Do not use unrefined oils, such as extra virgin olive oil. These contain monoglycerides, which may help to separate the mixture.

For best results and full flavor, fresh lemon juice should be used rather than bottled. Never whisk a raw egg into the cooked mixture in an effort to save it.

COLESLAW

To reduce calories, reduced-fat mayonnaise, nonfat yogurt and skim milk may be substituted for the ingredients listed.

3/4 cup mayonnaise

1/4 cup plain yogurt

2 tablespoons milk

1 1/2 teaspoons lemon-pepper seasoning

6 cups shredded cabbage (1/2 large head)*

2 medium carrots, shredded

3 small scallions, thinly sliced

1 teaspoon celery seed

❶ In small bowl, combine mayonnaise, yogurt, milk and lemon-pepper seasoning; mix well. Set aside.

❷ In large bowl, toss cabbage, carrots, 2 of the sliced scallions and celery seed. Pour mayonnaise mixture over cabbage mixture; toss gently.

❸ Sprinkle with remaining scallion. Cover with plastic wrap and refrigerate 2 hours before serving.

TIP *As a timesaver, use the packaged shredded cabbages now available in the produce section of supermarkets.

4 to 6 servings.

Preparation time: 15 minutes.
Ready to serve: 30 minutes.

Per serving: 360 calories, 34 g fat (5.5 g saturated fat), 25 mg cholesterol, 415 mg sodium, 3.5 g fiber.

CAESAR SALAD

Caesar Salad was created in the 1920's by Chef Caesar Cardini. The original Caesar salad did not contain any anchovies. It was simply romaine lettuce tossed with top-quality ingredients: extra-virgin olive oil, salt, fresh ground pepper, fresh lemon juice, a few drops of Worcestershire sauce, raw eggs, Parmesan cheese, then topped with croutons. Because of the fear of bacterial growth and contamination, a cooked Caesar dressing is now widely used.

1 head romaine lettuce, torn into 1-inch pieces

6 anchovies, chopped*

2 cups croutons

1/4 cup (1 oz.) freshly grated Parmesan cheese

1/2 cup *Cooked Caesar Salad Dressing* (page 130)

❶ Place greens in large bowl; add anchovies, croutons and Parmesan cheese. Pour dressing over salad; toss gently. Serve immediately.

TIP *Anchovies may be omitted.

4 servings.

Preparation time: 10 minutes.
Ready to serve: 15 minutes.

Per serving: 330 calories, 26.5 g fat (6 g saturated fat), 90 mg cholesterol, 470 mg sodium, 3 g fiber.

CAESAR SALAD

BLENDER MAYONNAISE

This is quickly prepared in the blender. If mayonnaise starts to curdle, add 1 tablespoon hot water while blending.

1   pasteurized egg

2   tablespoons white vinegar

1/2 teaspoon salt

1/2 teaspoon Dijon mustard

     Dash cayenne pepper

1   cup peanut or vegetable oil

❶ In blender, combine egg, vinegar, salt, mustard and cayenne pepper. Cover and blend at high speed 5 to 6 seconds.

❷ While motor is running, add oil in slow steady stream. Blend until thick and blended.

❸ Transfer to clean dry container. Refrigerate until needed.

1 1/3 cups.

Preparation time: 5 minutes.
Ready to serve: 5 minutes.

Per serving: 95 calories, 10.5 g fat (2 g saturated fat), 10 mg cholesterol, 60 mg sodium, 0 g fiber.

COOKED CAESAR SALAD DRESSING

Traditionally, raw or coddled eggs (cooked 1 minute) are used for Caesar salad. However, for complete safety, a cooked version is offered here.

2   egg whites

4   tablespoons fresh lemon juice

1/4 teaspoon dry mustard

1/4 teaspoon sugar

1/4 teaspoon hot pepper sauce

1/2 teaspoon garlic powder

1/2 cup peanut oil

❶ In small saucepan, whisk together egg whites, lemon juice, mustard, sugar, hot pepper sauce and garlic powder over low heat. Stir constantly until mixture thickens. Remove from heat.

❷ Set saucepan over ice water 1 minute to stop cooking. Let stand at room temperature 5 minutes.

❸ Transfer to large bowl; slowly whisk in oil.

❹ Serve at room temperature or chill until needed.

2/3 cup.

Preparation time: 5 minutes.
Ready to serve: 18 minutes.

Per serving: 100 calories, 11 g fat (2 g saturated fat), 40 mg cholesterol, 5 mg sodium, 0 g fiber.

VINAIGRETTE DRESSING

Use a combination of virgin olive oil (paler in color and flavor than extra virgin) and vegetable oils to prepare this light-tasting dressing. It keeps well in the refrigerator. Bring to room temperature before using, or zap in the microwave 10 seconds or so. Shake well before using. Add only enough dressing to very lightly coat each salad leaf.

- 1/4 cup cider vinegar
- 3 tablespoons fresh lemon juice
- 1/4 scant teaspoon jalapeño-flavored hot pepper sauce
- 1/2 teaspoon salt
- 1/4 cup virgin olive oil
- 1/4 peanut or other vegetable oil

❶ In small bowl, whisk together vinegar, lemon juice, hot pepper sauce and salt.

❷ Gradually pour in olive oil, then vegetable oil, whisking constantly until blended and thickened. Serve at room temperature.

3/4 cup.
Preparation time: 5 minutes.
Ready to serve: 5 minutes.

Per serving: 160, 18 g fat (3 g saturated fat), 0 mg cholesterol, 195 mg sodium, 0 g fiber.

Vinaigrette dressing is basically oil and vinegar with herbs and seasonings to flavor.

The usual proportion for a vinaigrette is 3 parts oil to 1 part vinegar, but feel free to experiment.

Make your own vinaigrette by varying oils and seasonings. Chopped herbs, garlic, pureed anchovies or other seasonings may be added as desired, and a mixture of oils may be used, as in this recipe.

TOSSED GREENS

While living in Switzerland, I found that in many homes, the vinaigrette ingredients are mixed at the bottom of a wooden salad bowl. Greens are torn into bite-size pieces, fresh herbs snipped with scissors and piled on top. Prepared this way, this salad may be covered and refrigerated up to 2 hours and then tossed at the table.

- 1 garlic clove, halved
- 8 cups mixed greens, torn into bite-size pieces
- 1/2 cup chopped fresh dill*
- 1/2 cup chopped fresh cilantro
- 1 cucumber, unpeeled, diced
- 1/3 cup *Vinaigrette Dressing* (left)

❶ Rub bottom and sides of salad bowl with cut side of garlic. Discard garlic.

❷ Add greens, dill, cilantro and cucumber; pour Vinaigrette Dressing over greens, tossing gently. Serve immediately.

TIP *Keep a pair of kitchen scissors on hand. They're useful for snipping fresh herbs right into the salad bowl so there's no messy cleanup.

4 servings.
Preparation time: 10 minutes.
Ready to serve: 10 minutes.

Per serving: 105 calories, 8.5 g fat (1 g saturated fat), 5 mg cholesterol, 205 mg sodium, 3 g fiber.

Salads are now available at supermarket salad bars. Prepared at home, however, it's much less expensive, and you have total control over seasonings and additives.

To avoid discoloration, never cut salad greens except when the recipe specifically calls for shredding or cutting into wedges, or the greens are to be used within the hour.

EGG SALAD

Everyone needs a good egg salad recipe.

- 1 rib celery, cut into 1-inch pieces
- 1 teaspoon dried onion
- 6 hard-cooked eggs, quartered
- 1/3 cup mayonnaise
  Dash cayenne pepper
- 1/4 teaspoon salt

❶ In food processor, coarsely chop celery and onion. Add eggs; process until mixture is finely chopped.

❷ Transfer to small bowl. Stir in mayonnaise, cayenne and salt. Garnish with parsley. Serve chilled.

2 cups.

Preparation time: 15 minutes.
Ready to serve: 1 hour.

Per serving: 125 calories, 11 g fat (2 g saturated fat), 165 mg cholesterol, 175 mg sodium, 0 g fiber.

VARIATION **New Fashioned Egg Salad**
Add 4 egg whites to 2 tablespoons reduced-fat mayonnaise and 2 tablespoons reduced-fat ricotta cheese. Add 1 rib celery (cut into 1-inch pieces) and 1/4 large red bell pepper (cut into 3 or 4 pieces). Stir in 1 tablespoon reduced-fat sour cream to enrich the mixture, imparting a home-style taste and texture.

COMPOSED FRUIT SALAD

A composed salad is, as the name suggests, an attractive arrangement of ingredients, with an accessorized dressing. Rose's Lime Juice Cordial, an intensely sweet and tart, nonalcoholic liqueur, is an essential ingredient in the watermelon dressing. It's used in cocktails, such as margaritas, and is available in liquor stores and supermarkets.

DRESSING
- 1/4 cup walnut oil
- 1/4 cup Rose's Lime Juice Cordial
- 1/4 cup seeded diced watermelon
- 2 tablespoons powdered sugar

SALAD
- 2 bananas
- 1 tablespoon fresh lemon juice
- 2 kiwi fruit, quartered
- 4 lychees
- 4 fresh pineapple rings
- 1 papaya, quartered, seeded

❶ In blender, combine walnut oil, lime juice cordial, watermelon and sugar. Blend 12 seconds; set aside.

❷ Cut bananas in half, then in half again lengthwise. Brush with lemon juice.

❸ Arrange attractively on each of four dessert plates: 2 pieces kiwi fruit, 1 lychee, 1 pineapple ring with 2 pieces banana inserted through and 1/4 papaya. Cut a small slice from bottom of papaya so it stands firmly on plate.

❹ Pour 1 to 2 teaspoons dressing into each papaya cavity. Drizzle remainder around fruits on plates or pass in small pitcher.

4 servings.

Preparation time: 10 minutes.
Ready to serve: 25 minutes.

Per serving: 340 calories, 15 g fat (1.5 g saturated fat), 0 mg cholesterol, 10 mg sodium, 6.5 g fiber.

Lychees are in season in June and July. Remove the bright red shell; the inside flesh is creamy white, satin smooth and sweet, surrounding a large dark seed. Canned lychees are available year-round, or a tiny bunch of seedless grapes may be substituted.

COMPOSED FRUIT SALAD

SUMMER SEAFOOD SALAD

A combination of tiny shrimp and summer vegetables presented in red cabbage leaf cups is elegant enough for a luncheon on the patio or a warm-weather supper. Serve with a basket of warm crusty rolls, a pot of sweet butter and a bottle of your favorite chilled white wine.

- 1 (7-oz.) pkg. frozen baby shrimp, thawed
- 6 new red potatoes, unpeeled, cooked, diced
- 1 medium yellow zucchini, cut into matchstick-size pieces
- 1/2 ripe pear, diced
- 2 tablespoons chopped red onion
- 2 tablespoons chopped fresh cilantro
- 1/4 cup *Vinaigrette Dressing* (page 131)
- 1/8 teaspoon salt
- 1/8 teaspoon freshly ground pepper
- 4 to 6 red cabbage leaf cups

❶ In medium bowl, combine shrimp, potatoes, zucchini, pear, onion and cilantro. Pour dressing over salad ingredients; toss gently to mix. Season with salt and pepper.

❷ Divide evenly among cabbage leaf cups. Serve chilled or at room temperature.

4 to 6 servings.

Preparation time: 25 minutes.
Ready to serve: 25 minutes.

Per serving: 270 calories, 7 g fat (1 g saturated fat), 85 mg cholesterol, 810 mg sodium, 5 g fiber.

ASIAN SLAW

Bok choy quickly becomes soggy when combined with dressing and refrigerated, even for a short time. So pour the dressing over and toss at the table, just before serving.

DRESSING
- 1/2 cup fresh lime juice
- 1/2 cup rice vinegar
- 2 tablespoons low-sodium soy sauce
- 2 tablespoons cilantro
- 1 tablespoon ginger-garlic puree*
- 2 teaspoons sugar
- 1 cup olive oil

SALAD
- 8 cups shredded bok choy
- 3 sliced scallions
- 1/2 cup roasted sunflower seeds
- 3 tablespoons toasted sesame seeds

❶ In food processor, combine lime juice, vinegar, soy sauce, cilantro, ginger-garlic puree and sugar. Process 10 seconds or until cilantro is finely chopped.

❷ With motor running, gradually pour in olive oil; blend about 12 seconds or until creamy. Makes about 2 cups.

❸ In large bowl, toss bok choy, scallions and sunflower seeds. Just before serving, shake vigorously. Pour dressing over salad; toss gently. Sprinkle with sesame seeds.

TIP *You can substitute 2 teaspoons fresh grated ginger and 1 teaspoon minced garlic for the ginger-garlic puree.

4 to 6 servings.

Preparation time: 20 minutes.
Ready to serve: 25 minutes.

Per serving: 660 calories, 66 g fat (8.5 g saturated fat), 0 mg cholesterol, 750 mg sodium, 4.5 g fiber.

Bok choy, or Chinese white cabbage, looks like a bunch of celery with leafy wide leaves. The taste is mild and the leaves are crunchy. Bok choy adds a refreshing contrast and texture to salads, vegetable mixes and stir-fries.

SANDWICHES

"Sandwich" may mean "white bread and bologna" to some people. But the word "sandwich" can also make your stomach rumble with hunger and your tastebuds start working overtime in anticipation ... if you're serving one of the sandwich recipes to come.

SANDWICHES

ESSENTIAL

SUBMARINE SANDWICH

"Submarine" is just one of the names for this colossal sandwich. Depending on your geographic area, it may be called a hero, grinder, hoagie or po'boy. Make a couple and you have a perfect crowd-pleaser. Filling may be thin-sliced meats, marinated vegetables, pickles, cheeses, cucumbers, salad greens or whatever is available. Toast the soft bread and make bread crumbs. Freeze and use as needed. Pickled mixed vegetables are available in a jar. Here's one version. Take it and experiment; every result is sure to be grand!

1	lb. Italian or French bread
1	cup pickled mixed vegetables, chopped
3	tablespoons mustard
6	oz. sliced ham
2	cups shredded lettuce
1	medium Vidalia onion, thinly sliced
6	oz. thinly sliced salami
6	oz. sliced provolone cheese
1/2	cup salsa

1. Split loaf in half lengthwise. Remove soft bread, leaving about 1-inch shell. Reserve bread for bread crumbs. Set aside.

2. In large bowl, mix pickled vegetables with mustard. Spread over bottom half of loaf.

3. Arrange sliced ham over mustard layer. Cover with lettuce and onion. Top with salami and cheese. Drizzle with salsa.

4. Replace top half of loaf, pressing down lightly. Slice diagonally.

6 servings.

Preparation time: 15 minutes.
Ready to serve: 15 minutes.

Per serving: 405 calories, 18.5 g fat (9 g saturated fat), 60 mg cholesterol, 1490 mg sodium, 3.5 g fiber.

REUBEN SANDWICH

The caraway seeds add a subtle anise flavor to the sauerkraut. However, if preferred, caraway may be omitted.

2	cups sauerkraut, drained
1	teaspoon caraway seeds
8	slices rye bread
1/4	cup vegetable oil
4	tablespoons horseradish mustard
3/4	lb. lean corned beef
1/3	cup Russian dressing
4	(3/4-oz.) slices Swiss cheese

① Heat oven to 425°F.

② In medium bowl, toss sauerkraut with caraway seeds. Set aside.

③ Arrange bread slices on baking sheet. Spray or brush both sides of bread with vegetable oil.

④ Spread 4 slices of bread each with 1 tablespoon mustard. Divide corned beef evenly and arrange over mustard. Spread dressing over mustard, then add 1/2 cup sauerkraut to each sandwich; top with 1 slice cheese.

⑤ Cover with remaining bread slices; press lightly.

⑥ Bake 7 or 8 minutes per side or until crisp and browned. Serve hot.

4 servings.
Preparation time: 10 minutes.
Ready to serve: 25 minutes.

Per serving: 575 calories, 33.5 g fat (9.5 g saturated fat),
75 mg cholesterol, 2585 mg sodium, 6.5 g fiber.

VARIATION **Open-Faced Reuben Sandwich**
Omit top slice of bread. Place under broiler to melt cheese. Sprinkle with a little paprika before serving.

The Reuben sandwich is allegedly named for Arthur Reuben, owner of a once-famous New York delicatessen (now out of business).

SLOPPY JOES

Here's a quick and easy weeknight supper. Any combination of ground beef, turkey or pork may be substituted. Ground turkey or ground pork contains less fat than ground beef; if these meats are used alone, add two extra tablespoons oil to recipe.

1	tablespoon vegetable oil
1/2	lb. lean ground beef
1/4	lb. ground turkey
1	small onion, chopped
1/4	cup steak sauce
1	(14.5-oz.) can Italian-flavored chopped tomatoes
1/8	teaspoon salt
1/8	teaspoon freshly ground pepper
4	kaiser rolls, split, toasted

① In medium saucepan, heat oil over medium heat until hot. Add ground beef, turkey and onion. Cook, stirring often, about 8 minutes or until meat is brown.

② Add steak sauce and tomatoes. Simmer, uncovered, 15 to 20 minutes or until slightly thickened. Season with salt and pepper.

③ Spoon over both halves of kaiser rolls. Serve hot.

4 sandwiches.
Preparation time: 5 minutes.
Ready to serve: 35 minutes.

Per serving: 390 calories, 17 g fat (5 g saturated fat),
50 mg cholesterol, 1415 mg sodium, 3 g fiber.

STYLISH HAMBURGERS

The all-American hamburger is basic—just ground beef and simple seasonings. But add a little onion, parsley and barbecue sauce to boost the flavor, and this old essential becomes a little more stylish. For a change, serve on garlic toasted crusty rolls, or go Italian and sandwich the hamburger in warm focaccia bread.

1¼ lb. lean ground chuck
¼ cup chopped onion
2 tablespoons finely chopped fresh parsley
2 tablespoons barbecue sauce
½ teaspoon salt
3 tablespoons oil
4 warm crusty rolls, split
1 cup baby lettuce
4 slices tomato

❶ In large bowl, combine beef, onion, parsley, barbecue sauce and salt. Shape into 4 (¾-inch-thick) patties. Set aside.

❷ Heat oil in large skillet over medium-high heat until hot. Cook patties 3 to 4 minutes per side or until no longer pink in center.

❸ Place patties on rolls; top with lettuce and tomato.

4 servings.
Preparation time: 10 minutes.
Ready to serve: 20 minutes.

Per serving: 525 calories, 29 g fat (8 g saturated fat), 85 mg cholesterol, 700 mg sodium, 2.5 g fiber.

To broil instead of fry, place patties on a greased rack of broiler pan. Broil about 4 inches from heat, 4 to 5 minutes per side for medium doneness or 5 to 6 minutes for well done.

MASTER
MUFFULETTA

A New Orleans specialty, muffuletta is a hollowed-out round loaf stuffed with piquant layers of roasted vegetables, meats and cheeses. Muffuletta is best made ahead of time. Wrap and refrigerate to allow time for ingredients to blend, and the bread to absorb flavors. Cut into wedges to serve. If you don't have time to make bread crumbs with the soft bread, place in a resealable plastic bag, tie and freeze.

1 (1-lb.) crusty round loaf bread
¼ cup olive oil
Dash dried oregano
4 oz. roasted red bell peppers
4 (1-oz.) slices mozzarella cheese
3 thin slices Vidalia onion
2 tablespoons capers, drained
8 slices kielbasa, thinly sliced

❶ With serrated knife, cut off top third of bread loaf. Pull out soft bread from bottom loaf, leaving about ¾-inch shell.

❷ Spray or brush inside of shell with olive oil. Sprinkle lightly with oregano.

❸ Arrange one-half of the roasted peppers in one layer on bottom of bread shell. Top with cheese, then onion. Sprinkle with capers. Cover with sausage, overlapping slices to fit. Top with remaining peppers; sprinkle lightly with olive oil and oregano.

❹ Replace top and press firmly. Wrap tightly in plastic wrap; refrigerate 1 hour.

❺ Cut into wedges to serve.

4 servings.
Preparation time: 20 minutes.
Ready to serve: 1 hour, 20 minutes.

Per serving: 400 calories, 24.5 g fat (6 g saturated fat), 25 mg cholesterol, 795 mg sodium, 2.5 g fiber.

MINER'S PASTIES

Pastry turnovers stuffed with leftover meats and vegetables were baked by Welsh housewives to satisfy lunchtime appetites of their coal-miner husbands. Instead of the usual beef and vegetables, these pasties are stuffed with a tarragon-flavored chicken and cheddar cheese mixture.

FILLING
- 1 tablespoon vegetable oil
- 1/2 cup chopped onion
- 3/4 cup frozen peas and carrots
- 1 1/2 cups finely chopped cooked chicken
- 3/4 cup (3 oz.) shredded sharp cheddar cheese
- 1 teaspoon dried tarragon
- 1/4 teaspoon salt
- 1/8 teaspoon freshly ground pepper

PASTRY
- 1 (17.3-oz.) pkg. frozen puff pastry sheets, thawed
- 1 egg, beaten

❶ Heat oven to 400°F. Spray 2 baking sheets with nonstick cooking spray.

❷ To prepare filling, heat oil over medium heat until hot in medium saucepan. Sauté onion, peas and carrots 4 to 5 minutes or until onion is tender and vegetables are thawed. Remove from heat. Add chicken, cheese and tarragon; season with salt and pepper. Set aside.

❸ On floured board, roll out one puff pastry, 1/8 inch thick. Cut out circles with 5 1/2- or 6-inch cutter.

❹ In center of each circle, place 1/4 cup filling. Moisten halfway around edge of each pastry circle with a little water. Fold pastry over to cover filling. Press with fork tines or crimp with fingers to seal. Brush with egg. Make 2 small cuts in pastry with sharp knife for steam to escape.

❺ Repeat with second puff pastry sheet and remaining ingredients.

❻ Place pasties on baking sheets. Bake 20 to 25 minutes or until puffed and golden brown. Serve warm or at room temperature.

8 (6-inch) pasties.

Preparation time: 10 minutes.
Ready to serve: 1 hour.

Per serving: 385 calories, 30 g fat (10.5 g saturated fat), 55 mg cholesterol, 255 mg sodium, 1 g fiber.

VARIATION **Traditional Pasties**
Instead of chicken and cheese, use 1 1/4 cups cooked ground or chopped beef. Substitute 2 teaspoons dried parsley for the tarragon.

CALIFORNIA WRAP

Warm tortillas in the microwave so that they are more pliable and more easily rolled. Here's how: Wrap 4 stacked tortillas loosely in damp paper towels. Microwave on High power for 10 to 15 seconds. Do not overheat or they will become leathery.

4	(8-inch) flour tortillas
4	rounded tablespoons chive-flavored cream cheese, softened
4	tablespoons canned chopped mild chiles
6	oz. thinly sliced smoked turkey
4	tablespoons chopped sun-dried tomatoes packed in oil
1	avocado, seeded, thinly sliced
1½	cups fresh alfalfa sprouts

❶ Spread each tortilla with 1 tablespoon of the cream cheese. Sprinkle 1 tablespoon of the chiles over each tortilla. Top with 1½ oz. of the sliced turkey and 1 tablespoon of the sun-dried tomatoes. Divide avocado evenly; arrange over sun-dried tomatoes. Sprinkle with alfalfa sprouts.

❷ Roll up tightly as for jelly roll.

❸ If to be refrigerated, wrap in plastic wrap.

4 servings.
Preparation time: 10 minutes.
Ready to serve: 10 minutes.

Per serving: 330 calories, 17.5 g fat (5.5 g saturated fat), 35 mg cholesterol, 895 mg sodium, 4.5 g fiber.

Tortillas are a round, thin, flat Mexican bread, now available in packages in most supermarkets. Corn and/or flour tortillas are used for traditional Mexican dishes such as burritos and tacos. Because they are low in calories, they have become the base for trendy wraps.

MASTER

PORTOBELLO MUSHROOM SANDWICH

Broiled portobello mushroom caps take the place of bread in this bright and tasty sandwich—an appealing meal for vegetarians, or anyone wanting to shy away from meat for a meal.

8	portobello mushroom caps
¼	cup olive oil
⅛	teaspoon salt
⅛	teaspoon freshly ground pepper
4	(1-oz.) slices smoked gouda cheese
4	tablespoons *Fresh Herb Pesto* (page 50)
4	thick slices tomato

❶ Heat broiler. Spray 15x10x1-inch baking sheet with nonstick cooking spray.

❷ Place mushroom caps, frilly side up, on baking sheet. Brush or spray with olive oil. Season lightly with salt and pepper. Broil 3 minutes.

❸ Place 1 slice of the cheese on top of each of 4 mushroom caps. Spread each with 1 tablespoon of the Fresh Herb Pesto; top with 1 of the tomato slices.

❹ Return filled and unfilled mushroom caps to broiler. Broil an additional 3 to 4 minutes or until cheese begins to soften.

❺ Place 1 mushroom cap over each filled cap to make a sandwich. Serve hot or at room temperature.

4 sandwiches.
Preparation time: 5 minutes.
Ready to serve: 15 minutes.

Per serving: 355 calories, 31.5 g fat (9 g saturated fat), 30 mg cholesterol, 920 mg sodium, 2 g fiber.

SIDE DISHES

Side dishes don't get any respect. And that's a shame. You work so hard to make the rest of a meal great, why give short shrift to a course that can really shine? Here are plenty of ideas to make your side dishes spectacular.

SIDE DISHES

Side dishes are an important part of any meal. They may consist of vegetables, grains, pasta or fruits. Nutritional guidelines recommend three to five servings of vegetables per day, and 6 to 11 servings of grains, pasta or bread. That's not difficult if you keep in mind that the recommended portion sizes are 1 cup raw leafy vegetables (as in salads), and ½ cup cooked or chopped raw vegetables.

Fresh vegetables are available in every supermarket, and farmers' markets are springing up in city locations. Now, most vegetables are available year-round, thanks to high-tech storage and transportation. Fresh asparagus, though expensive, may be served in winter or use frozen. While you can find a huge variety of leafy salad greens, many are pre-packaged, washed and ready to serve.

When serving grains or pasta, include vegetables. Peas may be added to cooked rice or mixed vegetables added to a package of prepared couscous. Not only does it provide good nutrition, these additions make for tastier, more exciting meals.

COOKING FRESH VEGETABLES

The three basic cooking methods for cooking fresh vegetables are:

1. Stovetop boiling
2. Stovetop steaming
3. Microwaving

Cooking times will vary depending on the age, size and amount of vegetables.

For stovetop boiling, leafy green vegetables cook quickly in a minimum amount of water. Boiling water prevents the nutritional content from leaching into the cooking liquid. Start timing as soon as the water returns to a boil. Check at minimum cooking time for crisp tenderness. Drain well in a colander. Add condiments and seasonings to taste.

Root vegetables should be placed in cold water. Bring to a boil, salt if desired, and start timing when water comes to a boil. Check for doneness at minimum cooking time. Drain well, add seasonings and condiments to taste.

Beets should never be peeled or scrubbed hard. If skin is damaged, the deep red color will be leached during cooking. Cover with boiling water. Add 1 to 2 tablespoons white vinegar to preserve color.

To steam vegetables, place a steamer basket over a saucepan of boiling water. Add vegetables, cover and cook to desired doneness.

Microwave cooking is quick and easy while retaining maximum nutrition. The vegetables may

be cut into even-sized pieces and cooked in a microwavable serving dish.

Before cooking, use a fork to pierce whole, unpeeled vegetables such as potatoes to keep them from bursting during cooking. For leafy vegetables, add 2 to 3 tablespoons water per pound of vegetables, cover loosely, and cook according to the chart at right. Remove from oven when barely tender. Let stand 3 to 5 minutes to finish cooking.

For root vegetables, add ¼ cup water per pound of vegetable. Stalk vegetables such as corn on the cob and asparagus may be wrapped in damp paper towels before cooking instead of placed in a dish. Cooking times are approximate depending on the microwave wattage.

VEGETABLE COOKING CHART

GREEN VEGETABLES

VEGETABLE (1 LB.)	BOILING/STEAMING	MICROWAVING
Asparagus	4 to 6 minutes	3 to 4 minutes
Beans (green, yellow, purple)	10 to 15 minutes	8 to 12 minutes
Broccoli Spears	8 to 12 minutes	7 to 10 minutes
Brussels Sprouts	10 to 12 minutes	8 to 11 minutes
Cabbage (wedges)	10 to 14 minutes	10 to 12 minutes
Cabbage (shredded)	6 to 8 minutes	5 to 7 minutes
Cauliflower Florets	8 to 10 minutes	6 to 10 minutes
Corn on the Cob	5 to 7 minutes	3 to 5 minutes/ear
Corn Kernels	4 to 5 minutes	6 to 8 minutes
Leeks	10 to 12 minutes	6 to 8 minutes
Mushrooms (sliced)	4 to 5 minutes	3 to 4 minutes
Okra	8 to 10 minutes	5 to 7 minutes
Peas (shelled)	8 to 10 minutes	6 to 8 minutes
Spinach	3 to 5 minutes	2 to 3 minutes

ROOT VEGETABLES AND SQUASH

VEGETABLE (1 LB.)	BOILING/STEAMING	MICROWAVING
Beets (unpeeled, whole)	40 to 50 minutes	25 to 30 minutes
Summer Squash/Zucchini	3 to 6 minutes	4 to 6 minutes
Carrots, sliced	7 to 9 minutes	6 to 9 minutes
Onions (small)	15 to 20 minutes	7 to 11 minutes
Onions (large)	30 to 35 minutes	11 to 14 minutes
Parsnips (1-inch pieces)	7 to 9 minutes	8 to 10 minutes
Potatoes (2-inch pieces)	20 to 25 minutes	10 to 12 minutes
Pumpkin (1-inch pieces)	15 to 20 minutes	10 to 13 minutes
Rutabaga (1-inch pieces)	15 to 20 minutes	15 to 18 minutes
Winter Squash (1-inch pieces)	15 to 20 minutes	10 to 13 minutes

POLENTA

Polenta is coarse cornmeal or grits. It may be white, yellow or blue, depending on the variety of corn used. The texture may be fine or very gritty. For this traditional dish, the usual method is to slowly add the cornmeal to the boiling water. But it's difficult to avoid lumping, even though you whisk madly. Instead, try whisking the cornmeal into cold, salted water, as in this recipe.

3	cups water
1½	teaspoons salt
1	cup stone-ground cornmeal
2	tablespoons butter
⅛	teaspoon freshly ground pepper

❶ In medium saucepan, heat water and salt over medium heat. Sprinkle in cornmeal; bring to a boil, whisking constantly.

❷ Reduce heat. As mixture thickens, stir with wooden spoon. Simmer 15 minutes, stirring often, until mixture stiffens. Add butter; season with pepper. Serve hot.

4 to 6 servings.

Preparation time: 5 minutes.
Ready to serve: 30 minutes.

Per serving: 180 calories, 6.5 g fat (3.5 g saturated fat), 15 mg cholesterol, 915 mg sodium, 2.5 g fiber.

VARIATION Polenta with Tomato-Cheddar Crust
Spray baking pan with cooking spray. Spoon polenta into pan. Top with ½ cup shredded sharp cheddar cheese. Arrange 1 thinly sliced tomato on top; sprinkle with another ¼ cup cheese. Place under broiler to brown. Serve hot.

VARIATION Fried Polenta
Pour cooked polenta into loaf pan. Cover and refrigerate overnight. Cut into ¾-inch slices. Dust with seasoned bread crumbs. Fry in butter or oil until browned on both sides. Serve with maple syrup, chunky tomato sauce or salsa.

VARIATION Pine Nut Polenta
Add 3 tablespoons toasted pine nuts and ½ teaspoon dried rosemary to polenta mixture before it is completely thickened.

ESSENTIAL

OVEN-GRILLED VEGETABLES

Any seasonal vegetable may be cooked quickly in this manner. Oil, season and cook under the broiler. Finish off in the oven's residual heat.

2	red bell peppers, seeded, cut into 8 pieces
2	zucchini squash, trimmed, quartered lengthwise, halved crosswise
2	baby eggplants, trimmed, sliced
¼	cup olive oil
2	tablespoons minced garlic
2	tablespoons chopped fresh basil or 2 teaspoons dried
⅛	teaspoon kosher (coarse) salt

❶ Heat broiler. Spray 15x10x1-inch baking sheet with nonstick cooking spray.

❷ Arrange peppers, skin side up, squash and eggplant in one layer on baking sheet.

❸ In large cup, combine oil and garlic. Brush vegetables generously with oil mixture. Sprinkle vegetables with basil and salt.

❹ Place under broiler, 4 inches from heat. Broil 5 minutes or until vegetables are brown at edges. Turn off broiler.

❺ Let vegetables rest in oven an additional 5 to 10 minutes or until tender. Serve hot.

4 to 6 servings.

Preparation time: 10 minutes.
Ready to serve: 25 minutes.

Per serving: 210 calories, 14 g fat (2 g saturated fat), 0 mg cholesterol, 590 mg sodium, 7 g fiber.

VARIATION Grilled Vegetables with Rosemary
Brush generously with an herb-infused oil, such as rosemary after broiling vegetables. Scatter with fresh rosemary.

VARIATION Sesame Nut-Crusted Vegetables
Broil vegetables 3 to 4 minutes or until just brown. Sprinkle with 2 tablespoons sesame seeds mixed with 2 tablespoons ground nuts. Finish broiling, watching carefully to avoid scorching.

OVEN-GRILLED VEGETABLES

KASHA (BUCKWHEAT GROATS)

Kasha, an old Russian term for buckwheat groats, is a whole grain with a pronounced nutty flavor. Though usually thought of as a cereal, it is really an herb with triangular seeds. It is available in coarse, medium and fine grinds. Kasha may be cooked on the stovetop or in the microwave. Leftovers may be used to thicken soups or stews, or to complement a pilaf. Beef, chicken or vegetable broth may be used as the liquid.

1 cup kasha
1 egg, lightly beaten
2 cups hot reduced-sodium chicken broth
3 tablespoons margarine
1/8 teaspoon salt
1/8 teaspoon freshly ground pepper

❶ Heat medium nonstick skillet over high heat. In medium bowl, combine kasha and egg; mix well. Add kasha mixture to skillet. Cook, stirring constantly with wooden spoon, until grains are separated and dry.

❷ Remove from heat; add broth. Mix well.

❸ Reduce heat to low. Cover skillet; simmer 15 minutes or until liquid is absorbed.

❹ Stir in margarine. Season with salt and pepper.

4 servings.

Preparation time: 5 minutes.
Ready to serve: 25 minutes.

Per serving: 210 calories, 11 g fat (2 g saturated fat), 55 mg cholesterol, 1235 mg sodium, 2 g fiber.

VARIATION **Kasha Varnishkas**
Stir in 1 cup cooked farfalle (bow-tie pasta) into cooked kasha.

VARIATION **Kasha with Butternut Squash**
Add 1/2 cup pureed seasoned butternut squash to cooked kasha.

VARIATION **Kasha with Walnuts**
Omit margarine. Stir in 3 tablespoons walnut oil and 1/4 cup chopped toasted walnuts to cooked kasha.

MICROWAVE METHOD FOR KASHA:
1 cup water
1 teaspoon butter
1/4 cup kasha

1. In 2-cup glass container, microwave 1 cup water 1 1/2 minutes on High power or until boiling. Add 1 teaspoon butter and 1/4 cup kasha. Cover with plastic wrap; vent.

2. Return to a boil, cooking on High power 30 to 45 seconds. Cook at Defrost setting 4 1/2 minutes. Drain and serve.

MASHED POTATOES

Mashed potatoes are the all-time most popular side dish. Some people like them lumpy, and some like them smooth and creamy. No matter how they are prepared, mashed potatoes are a favorite comfort food. Just be careful not to overcook, or they'll become watery and tasteless. To reduce calories, use reduced-fat milk or skim milk, reduce butter or margarine usage, and watch portion sizes (dietary guidelines note that 1/2 cup = 1 serving). Boost flavor with the addition of fresh herbs and infused oils. See all the great variation ideas!

1½	lb. russet potatoes, thinly peeled
1	teaspoon salt, plus more to taste
¼ to ½	cup warm milk or half-and-half*
3 to 4	tablespoons butter
⅛	teaspoon freshly ground pepper

① Cut potatoes into 1½ inch pieces. In large saucepan, cover potatoes with water; add salt. Bring to a boil over high heat. Reduce heat to medium; boil 20 to 30 minutes or until tender.

② Drain well. Return to pan; shake over low heat until dry.

③ Add ¼ cup warm milk and butter. Mash with potato masher or whip in food processor for a creamier, fluffier mixture. Add additional milk or cream, if desired. Season with pepper and additional salt, if desired.

TIP *Warm liquids give a fluffier texture.

4 to 6 servings.

Preparation time: 10 minutes.
Ready to serve: 45 minutes.

Per serving: 230 calories, 9.5 g fat (6 g saturated fat), 25 mg cholesterol, 1035 mg sodium, 3 g fiber.

VARIATION **Garlic-Smashed Potatoes**
Sauté 1 rounded tablespoon chopped garlic in 1 tablespoon garlic-flavored oil. Add to potatoes before mashing.

VARIATION **Crispy-Onion Potatoes**
Top with thinly-sliced crisp fried onions.

VARIATION **Pimiento-Stuffed Potatoes**
Omit pepper. Fold in ¼ cup diced pimiento and 1 teaspoon lemon pepper seasoning to mashed potatoes.

VARIATION **Tandoori-Whipped Potatoes**
Omit butter, salt and pepper. Add 3 tablespoons plain yogurt and 1 teaspoon tandoori seasoning before whipping in food processor.

FAST FIESTA PLATTER

A variety of attractively arranged vegetables make this platter irresistible. Cook according to the times on the Vegetable Cooking Chart (page 145). Personalize your homemade vinaigrette, or add fresh herbs and spices to a purchased dressing. In a hurry? Use fresh, frozen or canned vegetables.

1   cup *Vinaigrette Dressing* (page 131)
1   tablespoon chopped fresh dill
1   tablespoon chopped fresh parsley
2   teaspoons finely shredded fresh basil
3   beets, cooked, sliced (1/4 inch thick)
1/2 lb. green beans, cooked
1   (10-oz.) pkg. frozen baby carrots, thawed, cooked
2   ears corn on the cob, cooked, cut into 2-inch pieces
1   bunch broccoli spears, trimmed, cooked

❶ In covered jar, shake salad dressing with dill, parsley and basil. Set aside.

❷ On large platter, arrange beets in overlapping design over center of platter. Arrange beans, carrots, corn on the cob and broccoli spears around center.

❸ Shake dressing before drizzling over vegetables. Refrigerate one hour before serving. If desired, heat vegetable platter in microwave on High power 3 to 4 minutes or until hot.

6 to 8 servings.

Preparation time: 30 minutes.
Ready to serve: 1 hour, 30 minutes.

Per serving: 255 calories, 17 g fat (2.5 g saturated fat), 5 mg cholesterol, 390 mg sodium, 6.5 g fiber.

SUMMER VEGETABLE AU GRATIN

Visit your local farmers' market—or your own garden—for summer's freshest bounty.

3   tablespoons cornmeal
2   tablespoons crumbled goat cheese
1 1/2 teaspoons Italian seasoning
1/4 cup plus 1 tablespoon olive oil
2   cups diced fennel
1   cup diced mushrooms
1/8 teaspoon salt
1/8 teaspoon freshly ground pepper
2   medium yellow zucchini, sliced (1/4 inch thick)
2   portobello mushrooms, sliced (1/4 inch thick)
2   tomatoes, sliced (1/4 inch thick)

❶ Heat oven to 350°F. Spray 10-inch gratin dish with nonstick cooking spray.

❷ In small bowl, combine cornmeal, goat cheese and Italian seasoning. Set aside.

❸ Heat 2 tablespoons olive oil in small skillet over medium heat. Sauté fennel and mushrooms about 5 minutes or until tender. Spread over bottom of casserole. Season with salt, pepper and one-half of the cornmeal mixture.

❹ Arrange zucchini, portobello mushrooms and tomatoes alternately in rows over fennel.

❺ Brush or spray generously with olive oil; season with salt, pepper and remaining cornmeal mixture. Drizzle any remaining oil over cornmeal mixture. Bake 40 minutes or until vegetables begin to brown at edges. Serve hot.

4 to 6 servings.

Preparation time: 30 minutes.
Ready to serve: 1 hour, 20 minutes.

Per serving: 250 calories, 19 g fat (3.5 g saturated fat), 5 mg cholesterol, 640 mg sodium, 4.5 g fiber.

NEAL'S MUSHROOM RISOTTO

We arrived late at night in the little town of Corning, New York but Neal Cornelius had laid on a sumptuous spread including risotto, which he whipped up before we had finished the first glass of wine. Made the traditional way, risotto is a "stand over the stove" dish, needing constant attention while broth is added ever so gradually. The pressure cooker is the magic appliance here, but follow the manufacturer's directions as each model varies. Arborio rice, with its high starch content, gives this classic the exquisite creamy texture. Pecorino-Romano is an aged, hard cheese made from sheep's milk.

1/4	cup dried porcini mushrooms
1	tablespoon olive oil
1	medium onion, chopped
1	cup each Arborio rice, coarsely chopped mushrooms
1/4	cup dry white wine
2	cups reduced-sodium vegetable broth
2	tablespoons chopped fresh mixed herbs
1/4	cup (1 oz.) grated pecorino-Romano cheese
1/8	teaspoon each salt, freshly ground pepper

❶ Soak porcini mushrooms in warm water to cover. Let stand about 20 minutes. Drain and coarsely chop. Set aside.

❷ Heat oil in pressure cooker on top of stove over medium-high heat until hot. Sauté onion 2 to 3 minutes or until transparent. Stir in rice; cook until golden.

❸ Add mushrooms, wine, broth and fresh herbs. Bring to a boil. Cover, lock lid and increase pressure. Adjust heat to low to stabilize. Cook 7 minutes according to manufacturer's directions.

❹ Remove from heat. Run under cold water to release lid. Stir in mushrooms. If there is residual liquid, cook an additional 3 to 5 minutes over low heat. Sprinkle with grated cheese. Season with salt and pepper.

4 to 6 servings.

Preparation time: 20 minutes.
Ready to serve: 45 minutes.

Per serving: 250 calories, 5.5 g fat (1.5 g saturated fat), 5 mg cholesterol, 1140 mg sodium, 1.5 g fiber.

SLIGHTLY SWEET SPINACH PIE

This free-form pie is delicious on its own as a supper dish, but it's especially good as a side dish with chicken or pork.
A jar of baby food butternut squash beats cooking the small amount needed for this recipe.

1 (10-oz.) pkg. frozen chopped spinach, thawed
1/2 cup part-skim ricotta cheese
1 (4-oz.) jar butternut squash baby food
2 eggs, lightly beaten
1/4 cup dried currants
3 tablespoons cinnamon sugar
4 sheets phyllo dough
1/4 cup margarine, melted
2 tablespoons ground almonds

① Heat oven to 350°F. Spray 9-inch pie pan with nonstick cooking spray.

② Place spinach in colander; squeeze out as much water as possible. Transfer to medium bowl. Add cheese, butternut squash, eggs, currants and 2 tablespoons cinnamon sugar; mix well to blend. Set aside.

③ Place one phyllo sheet on pie pan, allowing edges to hang over sides. Brush with melted margarine; sprinkle with 1 rounded teaspoon ground almonds. Repeat with remaining 3 sheets phyllo, brushing each with melted margarine and sprinkling with ground almonds.

④ Spoon spinach mixture into phyllo-lined pie pan. Fold overhanging phyllo over spinach mixture to cover. Brush with remaining melted margarine, sprinkle with remaining almonds and remaining tablespoon cinnamon sugar. Bake 30 minutes or until top is nicely browned.

8 servings.

Preparation time: 30 minutes.
Ready to serve: 1 hour.

Per serving: 180 calories, 9.5 g fat (2 g saturated fat), 60 mg cholesterol, 170 mg sodium, 1.5 g fiber.

VARIATION **Slightly Sweet Spinach-Pasta Pie**
Omit the ricotta. Stir in 1/2 cup coarsely chopped cooked noodles to spinach mixture.

Phyllo refers to the tissue-thin pastry sheets used in Greek sweet and savory dishes, one of the most popular being Baklava, the sweet nut-filled pastry. Phyllo is available in long, rectangular packages in the freezer section of supermarkets.

OVEN-ROASTED SPUDS

Ask for potatoes in an English pub and you'll get "spuds." Try herb-infused oil, such as garlic or rosemary, to enhance these crusty, quick-cooked potatoes.

10 to 12 medium new red potatoes, cut into
 1-inch pieces

1 tablespoon salt

1/4 cup olive oil

2 tablespoons chopped fresh rosemary
 or 2 teaspoons dried

1 tablespoon chopped fresh dill or
 1 teaspoon dried

1/8 teaspoon kosher (coarse) salt

1/8 teaspoon freshly ground pepper

1 Heat oven to 400°F. Spray 15x10x1-inch baking sheet with nonstick cooking spray.

2 In large pot, cover potatoes with water; add salt. Bring to a boil over high heat. Reduce heat to medium; boil 10 minutes or until tender. Drain.

3 Pour in olive oil, rosemary and dill. Toss gently to coat potatoes. Spread on baking sheet. Bake 5 minutes. Reduce heat to 375°F. Turn potatoes with spatula. Bake an additional 15 minutes or until potatoes are nicely browned and cooked through.

4 to 6 servings.

Preparation time: 20 minutes.
Ready to serve: 45 minutes.

Per serving: 355 calories, 14 g fat (2 g saturated fat), 0 mg cholesterol, 600 mg sodium, 5 g fiber.

Varieties differ from region to region, but it is a potato's starch content that determines its cooking quality. High-starch potatoes, such as Idaho, are ideal for baking and French fries. Red "new" potatoes are waxy and keep their shape during cooking; they are perfect for salads, boiling or oven-roasting.

The potato is a member of the nightshade family. Potatoes left too long in the light will begin to turn green. That green skin contains a substance called solanine, which may taste bitter, and if eaten in quantity, may cause illness. Cut the green parts away before cooking. The rest of the potato is edible and harmless.

Potatoes are one of the world's most important staple foods. Unfortunately, they are grossly misunderstood by dieters. A medium-size baked potato contains only 90 calories. The added calories come with toppings such as sour cream, butter and cheeses. Instead, try a spoonful of herb-flavored yogurt (plain low-fat yogurt with a spoonful of chopped herbs) or infused olive oils.

SOUPS

Soup is one of the most delightful foods you can create. Delightful from a cooking standpoint—it's always fun to bring all the elements together. And delightful from an eating standpoint too—who can resist the aroma of a house where soup is being cooked, setting up your tastebuds for the first (and last) spoonfuls of the warm and heartening creation.

SOUPS

Homemade soups are a blessing. If you're part of a busy family, have a career, are single or part of a couple, or a senior citizen, soups are a wonderful catch-all for ingredients from your pantry, refrigerator or freezer. Soups create a magnificent melding of flavors. Almost any vegetable, except beets, may be included in a vegetable soup. (Beets will turn the soup a deep red and are usually only used in a borscht.)

Soups are right on target for any season. Cool pureed fruit soups or chilled vegetable cream soups add appeal to summer menus. Rib-sticking soups may be one-dish meals on cold winter days or hearty, nutritious supper starters. It's no coincidence that second-day soups taste better; flavors and ingredients have had a chance to blend.

For convenience, double the recipes and freeze in serving-sized containers, ready to be heated and on the table within minutes. Soups should always be brought to a rolling boil before serving. Adjust seasonings when the soup begins to simmer. If too thick, dilute with broth or milk, depending on the recipe.

There are many prepared stocks and broths available in the supermarket. They come in various forms from canned to cubes, but are usually highly concentrated and heavy on sodium. Homemade stocks and broths may be tailored to taste and dietary needs, with seasonings added to taste, and fats and oils minimized.

When you're in a hurry, a pot of good soup is quick and easy. Store-bought convenience items may be elevated to near "from scratch" by adding a few root vegetables such as carrots and onions, some fresh or dried herbs and a splash of lemon juice. Simmer 30 minutes, strain and use as needed.

ESSENTIAL

CHICKEN STOCK

No need to use a whole chicken. Chicken pieces such as legs, thighs, necks or backs will also produce a good rich stock. Cooked chicken may be used to add body to soups or in main dish salads.

4	lb. chicken wings, backs, necks and/or bones
16	cups water
3	medium onions, quartered
3	large carrots, sliced (1/2 inch thick)
1	medium parsnip, sliced (1/2 inch thick)
2	ribs celery with leaves, sliced into 1-inch pieces
1	(3-inch) parsley root, cut into 1/2-inch pieces
2	bay leaves
1/2	teaspoon peppercorns
3	tablespoons dry white wine
1/8	teaspoon salt

❶ Rinse chicken parts and pat dry.

❷ Place chicken parts in large pot; add water. Bring to a boil over high heat, skimming off foam as it rises to surface. Reduce heat to low; skim surface.

❸ Add onions, carrots, parsnip, celery, parsley root, bay leaves and peppercorns. Simmer, partially covered, 3 to 4 hours, skimming surface occasionally.

❹ Stir in wine before removing from heat. Season with salt.

❺ Strain stock through fine mesh strainer. Refrigerate, uncovered, until thoroughly chilled, 6 to 8 hours or overnight. Remove and discard any fat that has solidified on top of stock.

3 quarts.

Preparation time: 25 minutes.
Ready to serve: 4 hour, 30 minutes.

Per serving: 25 calories, 1 g fat (.5 g saturated fat), 0 mg cholesterol, 640 mg sodium, 0 g fiber.

CHICKEN STOCK FROM SCRATCH

Chicken stock requires a few minutes to prepare, then a couple of hours to simmer. A long cooking time extracts the flavor, protein and gelatin from chicken bones— the foundation of rich stock. Use these tips to obtain rich, clear stocks.

PROPER POT

Stocks can be made in any large pot; however, the best ones are tall with narrow openings. This limits the amount of evaporation that occurs and forces the liquid to simmer through several layers of meat and bones for richer flavor. The recipe for stock can be increased to accommodate larger stockpots. A six-quart stockpot holds a single recipe with room to spare. If you have an eight- or 10-quart pot, you can easily double the recipe.

Skim off the scum.

SAVING BONES

You can collect uncooked chicken bones over time. Keep a resealable plastic bag in the freezer; whenever you work with chicken, save breast bones, rib bones, necks, gizzards, back bones, wings and wing tips until there is enough for a pot of stock. Or buy chicken bones and parts from butchers who trim their own chickens. In a pinch, you can also use a whole chicken.

Strain the stock.

MAKING STOCK

Start with Bones: Rinse excess blood from the bones, but save the skin—it adds flavor, and the fat it contains is removed before the stock is used. Place the bones in the stockpot and cover them with cold water—never use hot water. Slowly bring the mixture to a boil. As the water begins to simmer, impurities coagulate and form a scum on the surface. Skim off the scum as it appears.

Vegetables and Seasoning: Once the liquid is gently boiling and the scum is no longer rapidly forming, add the vegetables and seasonings but no salt. Salt is never used when making stock because the stock reduces as it cooks; any added salt would intensify in flavor. Simmer the stock gently; never let it come to a full boil or it will become cloudy. The bubbles should be constant but gentle, not vigorous.

Remove the fat.

Strain and Skim: When the stock has simmered long enough for the flavor to be extracted (3 to 4 hours), strain it twice to remove all particles. Put the stock in several smaller containers to chill it in the refrigerator. Chilling stock causes the fat to congeal on the surface.

Remove Fat and Taste Stock: Once the stock is chilled, remove the fat and taste the stock. A well-made stock should be strong-tasting, clear and slightly gelatinous. When it's chilled, it should wiggle like weak gelatin. If the stock tastes weak or is watery, bring it to a full boil and boil vigorously to reduce it and concentrate the flavor.

Slightly gelatinous chilled stock.

STORING STOCK

Store stock in the refrigerator for up to two days. For longer storage, freeze stock in one- or two-cup portions. Try freezing stock in resealable plastic bags—they lay flat in the freezer and take up very little space.

VEGETABLE STOCK

Vegetable stock is the liquid in which vegetables have been cooked. It is rich in valuable nutrients and may replace water in soups and vegetarian dishes.

3	medium onions, quartered
4	ribs celery, cut into 1-inch pieces
2	(2- to 3-inch) parsley roots, cut into 1-inch pieces
2	tablespoons olive oil
2	large leeks, sliced thick (white parts only)
3	large carrots, sliced (1/2 inch thick)
3	slices fennel (1/2 inch thick)
1/4	small yellow turnip, cut into 1-inch pieces
3	garlic cloves, halved
2 1/2	quarts cold water
2	tablespoons fresh lemon juice
1/8	teaspoon salt
1/8	teaspoon ground white pepper

❶ In food processor, coarsely chop onions, celery and parsley root.

❷ Heat oil in large pot over medium heat. Sauté onions, celery and parsley root 5 to 10 minutes or until onion is tender.

❸ Stir in leeks, carrots, fennel, turnip, garlic and water. Bring to a boil over high heat. Skim off any foam.

❹ Reduce heat to a simmer, cover and cook 1 to 1 1/2 hours, stirring occasionally. Stir in lemon juice and pepper.

❺ Strain through fine mesh strainer over large bowl, pressing as much liquid as possible from vegetables. Discard remaining vegetables.

❻ Cool quickly. Refrigerate up to 5 days, or freeze in plastic containers up to 3 months.

8 cups.

Preparation time: 20 minutes.
Ready to serve: 2 hours.

Per serving: 12 calories, 0 g fat (0 g saturated fat), 0 mg cholesterol, 540 mg sodium, 0 g fiber.

Depending on the vegetables cooked, the water from cauliflower and cabbage tends to be stronger than that from the sweeter flavored carrots and parsnips. Take into account the type of dish the stock is being used for. For example, an asparagus stock would marry well in a delicate cream sauce.

COURT BOUILLON (FISH STOCK)

Court bouillon is any liquid used for poaching seafood—it could be as simple as salted water, or water with lemon juice or vinegar, or a more flavorful version such as this.

- 1 lb. fish trimmings*
- 1 onion, studded with 4 whole cloves
- 2 ribs celery, cut into 1-inch pieces
- 2 thin slices unpeeled lemon
- 2 bay leaves
- 1 cup dry white wine
- 1 teaspoon salt
- 1½ quarts water

❶ Wash trimmings in cold water.

❷ Place in large saucepan with onion, celery, lemon, bay leaves, wine, salt and water.

❸ Simmer, partially covered, 30 minutes. Strain through fine mesh strainer. Cool quickly and refrigerate, or freeze to use as needed.

TIP *For fish stock in a hurry, in a stainless steel pan (so stock will not darken), combine 2 cups bottled clam juice, 1 cup water, 1 sliced carrot, 1 medium onion cut into quarters, 2 tablespoons fresh lemon juice and ½ teaspoon dried thyme. Cover and simmer 30 minutes. Makes ⅔ cup.

1½ quarts.
Preparation time: 15 minutes.
Ready to serve: 55 minutes.

Per serving: 10 calories, 0 g fat (0 g saturated fat), 5 mg cholesterol, 520 mg sodium, 0 g fiber.

> The best court bouillon is made from fish heads and trimmings from any white-fleshed fish. Supermarkets don't usually have these trimmings but they are available from specialty fish shops. Court Bouillon may be frozen 3 to 4 weeks. Do not refrigerate more than 2 days before using.

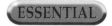

BEEF STOCK

Prepare this stock in the evening so that it can be checked during the long simmering process. Cooked beef may be chopped and added to make hearty vegetable soups.

- 3 lb. beef marrow bones
- 1 lb. beef ribs
- 1 large onion, quartered
- 4 whole cloves
- 1 (4-inch) parsley root, sliced (½ inch thick)
- 2 medium carrots, sliced (½ inch thick)
- 1 small white turnip, quartered
- 2 ribs celery, sliced (½ inch thick)
- 1 tablespoon salt
- 1 teaspoon dried thyme
- ½ teaspoon peppercorns
- 3 to 4 quarts water

❶ Place bones and ribs in large pot with boiling water to cover 5 minutes. Drain well, making sure all foam is poured off.

❷ Add onion, cloves, parsley root, carrots, turnip, celery, salt, thyme, peppercorns and water to cover. Simmer, partially covered, 3 to 4 hours.

❸ Remove from heat. Strain through fine mesh strainer. Cool stock quickly. Adjust seasonings, if desired.

❹ Refrigerate. Skim off fat from surface. Use as needed or freeze.

3 quarts.
Preparation time: 20 minutes.
Ready to serve: 4 hours, 20 minutes.

Per serving: 25 calories, 1 g fat (.5 g saturated fat), 0 mg cholesterol, 640 mg sodium, 0 g fiber.

> To avoid bacterial growth, cool stocks quickly in a large bowl or sink filled with ice water, stirring often. Refrigerate immediately.
>
> For stronger flavor, reduce by simmering, uncovered for an hour or so longer.
>
> For a quick fix, stir in a tablespoon or so beef bouillon granules. Stock keeps safely in refrigerator up to 5 days or in freezer up to 3 months. Bring to a rapid boil before using.

SWEET AND SOUR CABBAGE SOUP

My friend Fay learned this delicious Eastern European soup from her 90-year-old mother, Mrs. Sonnenschein. Nobody stops at just one bowl, which is why this recipe makes 12 hearty servings. Onions and cabbage may be coarsely chopped or shredded in the food processor, or buy cabbage already shredded. Beef granules reinforce the vegetable flavors. The recipe may be halved, if desired. Leftovers may be frozen.

2	tablespoons vegetable oil
3	large onions, coarsely chopped
1	teaspoon salt
1½	lb. cabbage, shredded
1	large carrot, shredded
2	tablespoons beef bouillon granules
1	(46-oz.) can tomato juice
1	(14.5-oz.) can Italian-style chopped tomatoes
3 to 4	bay leaves
	Juice of 3 large lemons
½	cup packed brown sugar
1	cup water
⅛	teaspoon ground white pepper

❶ In large pot, heat oil over medium heat. Add onions and salt. Cover; reduce heat to low. Cook, stirring often, 30 minutes or until onions are golden.

❷ Add cabbage, carrot and bouillon; stir to mix. Cook an additional 20 minutes or until cabbage is soft.

❸ Stir in tomato juice, tomatoes, bay leaves, lemon juice, brown sugar and water. Simmer, partially covered, an additional 30 minutes. Remove bay leaves. Season with pepper.

12 to 15 servings.

Preparation time: 20 minutes.
Ready to serve: 1 hour, 45 minutes.

Per serving: 125 calories, 3 g fat (0.5 g saturated fat), 0 mg cholesterol, 1340 mg sodium, 3 g fiber.

PENNSYLVANIA CHICKEN CHOWDER

A chowder is a thick, chunky soup usually containing seafood. Here we use chicken and bow-tie pasta, a favorite combination in the Pennsylvania Amish country.

  3 tablespoons oil
  1 small onion, chopped
  1 small red bell pepper, diced
  1 cup fresh or frozen corn kernels, thawed
  4$^{1}/_{2}$ cups reduced-sodium chicken broth
  1$^{1}/_{4}$ cups farfalle (bow-tie pasta)
  $^{1}/_{8}$ teaspoon saffron
  1 cup diced cooked chicken
  2 tablespoons chopped fresh parsley
  $^{1}/_{4}$ cup half-and-half
  1 hard-cooked egg, chopped

❶ In medium pot, heat oil over medium-high heat until hot. Sauté onion, bell pepper and corn 5 minutes or until onion is tender.

❷ Stir in broth, pasta and saffron. Cook, covered, 10 to 12 minutes or until pasta is al denté. Stir in chicken, parsley and half-and-half. Heat through. Do not boil.

❸ Spoon into bowls. Sprinkle with chopped egg.

4 to 6 servings.

Preparation time: 25 minutes.
Ready to serve: 50 minutes.

Per serving: 435 calories, 18 g fat (4 g saturated fat),
85 mg cholesterol, 1225 mg sodium, 3 g fiber.

FRUITED CABERNET BISQUE

A cool summer soup with pureed seasonal fruits. Substitute fruits as desired. Strawberries, blueberries and papaya may be used, depending on availability and taste.

  1 large ripe mango
  3 large apricots
  2 large ripe peaches
  2 black plums
  3 tablespoons honey
  $^{1}/_{2}$ cup cabernet wine
  2 cups apricot juice*
  8 to 10 mint leaves
  1$^{1}/_{2}$ tablespoons fresh lime juice

❶ Remove seeds from mango, apricots, peaches and plums. Cut into thin wedges. Set aside.

❷ In medium pan, warm honey over medium-high heat. Sauté prepared fruits 2 to 3 minutes.

❸ Stir in wine and juice. Reduce heat to medium. Simmer 10 minutes or until fruit is soft.

❹ Cool slightly before pouring into blender. Add mint leaves and lime juice; blend until smooth.

❺ Serve chilled or at room temperature. Garnish with drizzle of softly whipped cream.

TIP *If soup is too thick, add a little extra apricot juice bit by bit.

4 servings.

Preparation time: 15 minutes.
Ready to serve: 1 hour, 30 minutes.

Per serving: 170 calories, 0 g fat (0 g saturated fat), 0 mg cholesterol,
6 mg sodium, 4.5 g fiber.

FRUITED CABERNET BISQUE

GOLDEN MUSHROOM, BEEFSTEAK AND BARLEY SOUP

A thick, rib-sticking soup— hearty enough for a meal in a dish or served in smaller portions as a starter.
To speed things up, buy ready-sliced mushrooms, shredded carrots in a bag, and frozen baby onions
that are peeled and ready to use.

1	lb. beef chuck, trimmed
3	tablespoons all-purpose flour
1/8	teaspoon salt
1/8	teaspoon freshly ground pepper
2	tablespoons vegetable oil
1 1/2 to 2	quarts *Beef Stock* (page 160)
2	cups tiny baby onions
2	cups sliced mushrooms
1 1/2	cups shredded carrots
1	(10-oz.) pkg. frozen cooked squash, thawed
1/4	cup pearl barley
3	tablespoons Worcestershire sauce
1	teaspoon minced garlic
1/2	cup parsley sprigs

❶ Cut beef into 1/2-inch pieces. Dredge in flour. Season with salt and pepper.

❷ Heat oil in large pot over medium-high heat. Cook beef until edges just begin to brown.

❸ Add 1 1/2 quarts stock, onions, mushrooms, carrots, squash, barley, Worcestershire sauce and garlic. Bring to a rolling boil. Skim off any foam.

❹ Reduce heat to simmer. Cover and cook 1 hour, stirring often, or until meat is tender. Season with salt and pepper. If too thick, add a little extra stock.

❺ Stir in parsley just before serving.

4 to 6 servings.

Preparation time: 30 minutes.
Ready to serve: 1 hour, 45 minutes.

Per serving: 520 calories, 22.5 g fat (6.5 g saturated fat), 70 mg cholesterol, 860 mg sodium, 9.5 g fiber.

WHITE AND GREEN GAZPACHO

Inspired by the Spanish red liquid salad, this white variety includes jicama, which imparts a sweetness and slight crunchiness. The fresh green herbs, nuts and grapes are more than a garnish. They are an important part of the soup and should be stirred in by the diner right before eating.

6	small white potatoes, quartered
3	cups cold water
1	cup milk
1½	cups diced jicama
1½	tablespoons white vinegar
⅛	teaspoon salt
⅛	teaspoon freshly ground pepper
½	cup chopped fresh parsley
16	seedless green grapes, halved
2	tablespoons toasted slivered almonds

❶ Place potatoes in saucepan with 3 cups cold water. Bring to a boil over high heat. Reduce heat to a simmer. Cover and cook until potatoes begin to break up. Remove from heat. Cool slightly.

❷ Drain potato cooking liquid into measuring cup. Add enough milk to make 2¼ cups liquid.

❸ Transfer cooked potatoes, 2¼ cups liquid and jicama to blender. Blend at high speed 20 to 30 seconds or until smooth. Add vinegar; blend an additional 3 seconds. Season with salt and pepper. Refrigerate until ready to serve.

❹ In medium bowl, combine parsley, grapes and almonds. Refrigerate.

❺ When ready to serve, pour potato mixture into four bowls. Evenly divide parsley mixture and spoon over top of each portion.

4 servings.
Preparation time: 20 minutes.
Ready to serve: 1 hour, 15 minutes.

Per serving: 135 calories, 3 g fat (1 g saturated fat), 5 mg cholesterol, 620 mg sodium, 4.5 g fiber.

Jicama (Mexican potato) is a fat, bulbous-looking root vegetable. The thin brown skin must be peeled before using, and the white crunchy flesh has a sweet, nutty flavor. Jicama makes an excellent addition when thinly sliced in salads or cooked as a vegetable.

DESSERTS

What is life without dessert? Go ahead and indulge a little bit. It's good for the soul. Here are the building-block and master recipe ideas you need to create your best dessert sensations yet.

DESSERTS

Everybody loves dessert. Store-bought treats may look impressive, but rarely do they have that home-baked goodness, nor do they impart delicious smells from the kitchen while baking. And costwise, homemade is cheaper as well as better.

Desserts range from rich cakes and cookies to fruit compotes and flans. For success in baked goods, recipes must be followed exactly, for baking is a science. Take advantage of locally grown fruits in season. Crisp fall apples may be transformed into dumplings with your own filling. When you tire of eating fresh berries, transform them into compotes or fruit tarts. Essentials, such as pie crusts and graham-cracker crusts, may be pressed into pie pans and frozen, ready to pull out and fill as needed.

ESSENTIAL

CRUMB CRUST

A crust made from cookie crumbs is perfect for light, chiffon-like fillings, frozen cream pies and cheesecakes. The most popular crumb crusts are those made from graham crackers, but any crumbs may be used. Substitute vanilla wafer crumbs, chocolate wafer crumbs or shortbread crumbs. A crumb crust need not be baked, but I've found that brushing with lightly beaten egg white and baking before filling will help you slice the final creation cleanly without cracking or crumbling the crust.

- 1/3 cup butter, melted
- 1½ cups finely crushed cookie crumbs
- 4 tablespoons sugar
- 1 egg white

❶ Heat oven to 350°F. Spray 9-inch pie pan with nonstick cooking spray.

❷ In medium saucepan, melt butter over medium heat. Remove from heat. Stir in cookie crumbs and sugar; mix well.

❸ Spoon mixture into pie pan. With fingers, pat evenly and firmly over bottom and sides of pan.

❹ Refrigerate 20 minutes before brushing with egg white. Bake 8 to 10 minutes or until crust is firm to touch. Cool before filling.

1 pie crust.
Preparation time: 10 minutes.
Ready to serve: 1 hour.

Per serving: 205 calories, 12 g fat (7 g saturated fat), 25 mg cholesterol, 185 mg sodium, 0 g fiber.

ESSENTIAL

PIE CRUST PASTRY

This is enough for a 2-crust pie. When making a 2-crust pie, divide the dough into two portions, a larger portion for the bottom and sides of the pie dish, a smaller portion for the top.

- 2 cups all-purpose flour
- 3/4 teaspoon salt
- 1 cup plus 4 tablespoons unsalted butter, chilled, cut up
- 5 tablespoons ice water

❶ Mix flour and salt in food processor. Add butter; pulse until mixture crumbles.

❷ Gradually add 2 tablespoons cold water. Add enough remaining water to work dough into ball.

❸ Remove from food processor. Wrap in plastic wrap. Refrigerate 30 minutes before rolling out.

2 (9-inch) crusts

Preparation time: 35 minutes.
Ready to serve: 45 minutes.

Per serving: 490 calories, 39 g fat (24 g saturated fat), 105 mg cholesterol, 295 mg sodium, 1 g fiber.

Handle pastry lightly and little. You want to incorporate as much air as possible for manageable but flaky dough. If handled too much, the pastry will be tough. Chilled liquids, such as ice water, help keep the gluten from forming.

Weather and humidity affect flour absorption. When a range is given, always use the lesser amount of flour first, adding more if needed. Too much flour will make bread stiff and tough.

OLD-FASHIONED APPLE PIE

Here's your basic apple pie recipe to use with Pie Crust Pastry *(page 168). All-purpose Cortlands and Winesaps are good pie apples but almost any variety may be used. Golden Delicious apples are excellent for open tarts since they hold their shape through cooking. If apples are tart, increase the sugar in the recipe.*

1	recipe *Pie Crust Pastry* (page 168)
1/2	cup sugar
3	tablespoons cornstarch
2	teaspoons grated lemon peel
1	teaspoon cinnamon
6	large Golden Delicious apples
2	tablespoons butter
1	teaspoon water
1	tablespoon cinnamon sugar

❶ Heat oven to 400°F. Line 9-inch pie pan with Pie Crust Pastry.

❷ In large bowl, combine sugar, cornstarch, grated lemon peel and cinnamon; mix well. Set mixture aside. Peel and core apples, then slice 1/4 inch thick. Add to sugar mixture; toss to coat.

❸ Turn mixture into pan. Dot with butter. Cover with top pastry crust. Seal and flute with fingers or press edges firmly together with fork tines. Brush with water and sprinkle with cinnamon sugar. Cut three 1-inch steam vents in center. Bake 50 minutes or until pastry is golden and juice begins to bubble through steam vents. Cool on wire rack.

8 servings.

Preparation time: 45 minutes.
Ready to serve: 1 hour, 35 minutes.

Per serving: 450 calories, 22 g fat (13 g saturated fat), 55 mg cholesterol, 315 mg sodium, 4 g fiber.

STREUSEL MIX

Streusel means "sprinkle" in German. Streusel was originally a crumbly mixture of flour, sugar, butter and spices used as a topping for muffins and coffee cakes. There are dozens of variations, but this basic recipe can be mixed by hand in seconds—no need to use the food processor.

- 3/4 cup all-purpose flour
- 1/2 cup packed brown sugar
- 4 tablespoons unsalted butter, chilled
- 1 teaspoon powdered cinnamon

❶ In small bowl, mix flour and brown sugar.

❷ Cut in butter with pastry blender or fingers until mixture crumbles. Stir in cinnamon.

1 1/4 cups.
Preparation time: 5 minutes.
Ready to serve: 5 minutes.

Per serving: 195 calories, 8 g fat (5 g saturated fat), 21 mg cholesterol, 8.5 mg sodium, 0.5 g fiber.

VARIATION Oatmeal Streusel
Substitute 1/2 cup old-fashioned or quick-cooking oats and 1/4 cup all-purpose flour for 3/4 cup flour.

VARIATION Nut Streusel
Combine 1/2 cup coarsely chopped nuts with 1/4 cup all-purpose flour and 1/2 cup packed brown sugar. Cut in 4 tablespoons butter until mixture crumbles. Stir in 1/4 teaspoon each cinnamon and nutmeg.

VARIATION Cake-Crumb Streusel
Replace flour with 3/4 cup crumbled dry pound cake crumbs.

VANILLA BUTTER FROSTING

Homemade cakes and cookies deserve only the best toppings. Use butter, not margarine, for a rich and full flavor.

- 4 cups powdered sugar, sifted
- 6 tablespoons softened butter, cut into 6 pieces
- 1 teaspoon vanilla
- 5 tablespoons half-and-half

❶ In small bowl, mix powdered sugar, butter and vanilla with fork.

❷ With mixer at medium speed, beat in enough milk or half-and-half to make smooth, spreadable mixture.

2 cups.
Preparation time: 10 minutes.
Ready to serve: 10 minutes.

Per serving: 210 calories, 6 g fat (3.5 g saturated fat), 15 mg cholesterol, 40 mg sodium, 0 g fiber.

VARIATION Espresso Frosting
Substitute strong espresso coffee for milk or half-and-half. Omit vanilla.

VARIATION Maple Cream Cheese Frosting
Substitute maple flavoring for vanilla extract and 1 (3-oz.) pkg. softened cream cheese for the butter. Add enough milk or cream to make spreadable mixture. Refrigerate the frosted cake when using this recipe.

VARIATION Chocolate Cream Frosting
Beat in 1 (1-oz.) square unsweetened chocolate, melted, into butter mixture. Add 1 to 2 tablespoons cream to make the mixture spreadable.

VARIATION Almond-Flavored Frosting
Substitute almond extract for vanilla extract and 2 tablespoons almond-flavored liqueur for milk or half-and-half.

APPLE DUMPLINGS

Apple dumplings are simply peeled apples stuffed with dried fruits, spices and/or preserves, then wrapped in a pastry. Speed up recipe preparation by using store-bought frozen puff pastry, thawed and rolled out thinly. Apples may be peeled, cored and sliced, or cored and stuffed, as in the recipe below. Reduce cooking time by microwaving whole apples 1 to 2 minutes on high. Cool completely before wrapping with pastry.

DUMPLINGS

- 2 tablespoons chopped dried fruits
- 2 tablespoons chopped walnuts
- 2 tablespoons packed brown sugar
- 1/2 teaspoon cinnamon
- 4 apples, peeled, cored
- 1 recipe *Pie Crust Pastry* (page 168)

SAUCE

- 1/2 cup packed brown sugar
- 1/2 cup water
- 1 rounded teaspoon butter

❶ Heat oven to 375°F. Spray 3-quart casserole with nonstick cooking spray.

❷ In small bowl, combine dried fruits, walnuts, brown sugar and cinnamon. Set aside.

❸ On lightly floured surface, roll dough out to about 1/4 inch thickness. Cut into 4 squares.

❹ Set one apple in middle of pastry square. Stuff with 2 to 3 teaspoons of the dried fruit mixture. Bring pastry up and around to cover; pinch to seal.

❺ Repeat with remaining apples, pastry and fruit mixture. Place seam side down in casserole. Set aside.

❻ To prepare sauce, mix 1/2 cup brown sugar, water and butter in another small bowl. Microwave 1 minute on High power or until butter is melted. Stir to mix; pour over dumplings. Cover loosely with aluminum foil.

❼ Bake 40 minutes or until apples are tender and pastry is golden. Baste with sauce once or twice during baking.

4 servings.

Preparation time: 30 minutes.
Ready to serve: 1 hour, 10 minutes.

Per serving: 985 calories, 62 g fat (37 g saturated fat), 158 mg cholesterol, 465 mg sodium, 5 g fiber.

Apples are available all year, but some are better than others for specific cooking methods. The most popular found in supermarkets are the following:

Cortland and **Braeburn** are crisp with a slightly tart flavor. Considered good all-purpose apples, they are especially good for baking.

Golden Delicious have a yellow-gold skin and a slightly mealy texture. The older varieties have a pink blush, but they have a better flavor. They retain their shape during cooking, so they are good for open tarts and compotes where appearance is important. They also resist discoloration when exposed to air, making them a good choice to be served with cheeses.

Granny Smith, with apple-green skin and tart flesh, is the choice for dishes that call for a firm apple. They add a delightful crunchiness to Waldorf salads and combine beautifully with sweet chocolate, as in a chocolate fondue.

Jonathan and **McIntosh** are sweet, juicy and slightly mealy. Both are good eating apples and are excellent in cooking, as well as in salads and pies.

Red Delicious, with shiny red skin, are sweet, not very crisp and are best eaten out of hand. They fall apart easily during cooking.

How many apples do you need?
- 3 medium or 2 large apples = 1 pound = 2 3/4 cups sliced
- 3 medium grated apples = 1 1/2 cups

AUNT HANNI'S BLUEBERRY TORTE

Aunt Hanni is a marvelous baker who brought many of her recipes to America from Germany. This one, shared with her daughter Carol, is one of my husband's favorite desserts. Fresh blueberries are best, but in winter, with a little lemon juice added, frozen berries taste just as delicious.

CRUST

1/2	cup butter, softened
1/4	cup sugar
1	egg, beaten
1 1/2	cups all-purpose flour

FILLING

3/4	cup sugar
3	tablespoons cornstarch
1/8	teaspoon salt
1	cup water
1	quart fresh or frozen blueberries, thawed
2	teaspoons grated fresh ginger

❶ Heat oven to 350°F. Spray 10-inch springform pan with nonstick cooking spray.

❷ Cut butter into 6 or 8 pieces. Place in food processor with sugar, egg and 1/2 cup of the flour. Pulse 2 or 3 times to mix. Pulse, adding remaining 1 cup flour to form ball. Press dough into bottom of pan and 1 inch up sides; prick all over with fork.

❸ To keep bottom of pastry shell from rising during baking, cover pastry with sheet of aluminum foil weighted down with 2 cups of dried beans or rice. Bake 15 minutes or until edges just begin to brown. Remove dried beans and foil. Cool on wire rack.

❹ To prepare filling, combine sugar, cornstarch, salt and water in large saucepan. Bring to a boil over medium-high heat, stirring constantly. Cook 1 minute. Remove from heat; gently stir in blueberries and ginger. Cool before pouring into baked shell. Garnish with rosettes of whipped cream.

8 servings.

Preparation time: 25 minutes.
Ready to serve: 55 minutes.

Per serving: 275 calories, 10 g fat (6 g saturated fat), 46 mg cholesterol, 100 mg sodium, 2 g fiber.

Weighting down an empty pie crust to prevent the pastry from rising during baking is called baking "blind." Cover the bottom with aluminum foil or parchment paper and cover that with dried beans or uncooked rice.

When baking is completed, cool beans and store in a jar in a dry place. The beans may be used over and over again as pie weights.

SPRING FRUIT CRISP

If you feel adventurous, try some other fruits in this great crisp. But to start, the rhubarb and strawberries are wonderful. The topping for any fruit crisp is a streusel topping. Use the basic Streusel Mix *(page 170) or this richer version below.*

CRISP

2 cups diced rhubarb

2 cups strawberries, hulled

1 cup sugar

2 tablespoons all-purpose flour

1/8 teaspoon ground cloves

TOPPING

1 cup packed brown sugar

3/4 cup all-purpose flour

1/2 teaspoon cinnamon

Dash ground cloves

6 tablespoons butter, chilled

1/2 cup chopped pecans

❶ Heat oven to 350°F. Spray 9-inch square pan with nonstick cooking spray.

❷ In large bowl, toss rhubarb and strawberries with sugar, flour and cloves. Pour into pan. Set aside.

❸ In small bowl, mix brown sugar, flour, cinnamon and cloves. Cut in butter with pastry blender or fingers until mixture crumbles. Stir in pecans.

❹ Spread nut mixture over rhubarb and strawberries.

❺ Bake 45 minutes or until golden brown and bubbly.

8 servings.

Preparation time: 20 minutes.
Ready to serve: 1 hour, 5 minutes.

Per serving: 390 calories, 14 g fat (6 g saturated fat), 25 mg cholesterol, 70 mg sodium, 2.5 g fiber.

Mature rhubarb, with its thick, red sour stalks, is a member of the buckwheat family. Although it's usually eaten as a fruit, botanically it is a vegetable. The big, flat green leaves contain oxalic acid, which is toxic. Leaves should be removed and discarded before cooking. The stalks of rhubarb grown in hothouses are pale pink with much less flavor and tartness than the field-grown variety. In some areas, hothouse rhubarb is available year-round. Field-grown is available in late spring and early summer.

In Britain, the traditional flavoring for rhubarb jams and desserts is ground ginger, which may be used instead of cloves in this recipe.

MILE-HIGH LIME CHIFFON PIE

This impressive dessert is gussied up with mint sprigs and thinly sliced lime, or simply sprinkled with a little shaved chocolate. Substitute orange gelatin and frozen orange juice for the lime flavors. Garnish with orange peel, if you wish. Keep all the ingredients on hand for impromptu entertaining. After a brief chill in freezer, this light and airy concoction can be served up in no time!

- 1 (9-inch) chocolate cookie pie crust
- 1 egg white, lightly beaten
- 1 (6-oz.) pkg. lime-flavored gelatin
- 2 cups boiling water
- 1 (12-oz.) can frozen limeade
- 1½ (12-oz.) containers frozen whipped topping, thawed

❶ Heat oven to 375°F. Brush pie crust with beaten egg white. Bake 5 minutes. Cool completely. Turn off oven.

❷ In large bowl, combine gelatin with boiling water; stir to dissolve gelatin completely.

❸ Add frozen limeade; stir until limeade is dissolved. Place in refrigerator 2 hours to set. If freezing, stir once after 15 minutes. Remove when mixture is consistency of thick egg whites.

❹ Add one container of whipped topping. Whisk about 1 minute or until no green traces remain and mixture is smooth and creamy. Spoon into crust; refrigerate until set.

❺ Just before serving, gently spread remaining whipped topping over lime mixture. Garnish with mint sprig, lime peel or thinly sliced lime. Store pie in refrigerator.

8 to 10 servings.

Preparation time: 1 hour.
Ready to serve: 1 hour.

Per serving: 455 calories, 21 g fat (15 g saturated fat), 20 mg cholesterol, 195 mg sodium, 1 g fiber.

PEACHY RICE PUDDING

Whole milk and long simmering gives this rice pudding an irresistible, creamy texture. If fresh peaches are not available, use 1 cup canned diced peaches and 5 to 6 peach wedges to garnish. One-fourth cup granulated sugar and ¼ cup honey may be substituted for the maple syrup.

- ¾ cup long-grain rice
- ½ cup maple syrup
- 4 cups whole milk
- ¼ teaspoon salt
- 2 peaches, unpeeled, stones removed
- ⅛ teaspoon cinnamon

❶ In heavy saucepan, combine rice, maple syrup, milk and salt; cook over low heat. Bring to a simmer.

❷ Reduce heat. Cook, uncovered, 1¼ hours or until rice is tender, stirring frequently.

❸ Remove from heat; let stand 30 minutes.

❹ Cut one peach into ½-inch dice; fold into rice pudding.

❺ Transfer to serving bowl. Dust lightly with cinnamon. Cut remaining peach into thin wedges; arrange attractively over pudding. Serve warm, at room temperature or chilled. Store pudding in refrigerator.

6 servings.

Preparation time: 10 minutes.
Ready to serve: 2 hours.

Per serving: 265 calories, 5.5 g fat (3.5 g saturated fat), 20 mg cholesterol, 180 mg sodium, 1 g fiber.

RECIPE INDEX

This index lists every recipe in The Art of Cooking: Recipes & Techniques *by name. If you're looking for a specific recipe but can't recall the exact name, turn to the General Index that starts on page 179.*

GENERAL INDEX

There are several ways to use this helpful index. First—you can find recipes by name. If you don't know a recipe's specific name but recall a main ingredient or the cooking technique, look under that heading and all the related recipes will be listed; scan for the recipe you want. If you have an ingredient in mind and want to find a great recipe for it, look under that ingredient heading as well to find a list of recipes to choose from. Finally—you can use this general index to find a summary of the recipes in each chapter of the book (appetizers, soups, salads, desserts, side dishes, etc.).

COOKING REFERENCE CHARTS

These helpful charts of temperatures, equivalents, conversions and much more will come in handy for even the experienced cook.

RECOMMENDED INTERNAL COOKING TEMPERATURES
FROM THE U.S. FOOD AND DRUG ADMINISTRATION

Eggs	Cook until yolk and white are firm
Egg dishes	160°F
GROUND MEAT AND MEAT MIXTURES	
Turkey, Chicken	170°F
Veal, beef, lamb, pork	160°F
FRESH BEEF	
Rare (some bacterial risk)	140°F
Medium	160°F
Well done	170°F
FRESH VEAL	
Medium	160°F
Well done	170°F
FRESH LAMB	
Medium	160°F
Well done	170°F
FRESH PORK	
Medium	160°F
Well done	170°F
POULTRY	
Chicken, turkey, duck or goose	180°F
Thighs	Cook until juices run clear
Stuffing	165°F
HAM	
Fresh (raw)	160°F
Pre-Cooked	140°F
Shoulder	160°F
FISH	160°F (10 min./inch thick in 450°F oven)
Clams and oysters	Steam 6 to 8 minutes

MEASUREMENT EQUIVALENTS

16 tablespoons = 1 cup

12 tablespoons = ¾ cup

10 tablespoons plus 2 teaspoons = ⅔ cup

8 tablespoons = ½ cup

6 tablespoons = ⅜ cup

5 tablespoons plus 1 teaspoon = ⅓ cup

4 tablespoons = ¼ cup

2 tablespoons = ⅛ cup

2 tablespoons plus 2 teaspoons = ⅙ cup

1 tablespoon = 1/16 cup

2 cups = 1 pint

2 pints = 1 quart

3 teaspoons = 1 tablespoon

48 teaspoons = 1 cup

CUSTOMARY PAN SIZES

	SIZE	VOLUME
CAKE PANS		
Round	8x1½ inches	4 cups
	9x2 inches	6 cups
Rectangular	13x9x2 inches	15 cups
Square	8x2 inches	8 cups
	9x 1½ inches	8 cups
	9x2 inches	10 cups
Tube	9x3 inches	12 cups
	10x4 inches	18 cups
LOAF PANS	8½ x 4½ x 2½ inches	6 cups
	9x5x3 inches	8 cups
PIE PANS	8x 1¼ inches	3 cups (level)
	9x1½ inches	4 cups (level)
	9x2 inches	6 cups (level)
TART OR QUICHE PANS	4x 1¼ inches	½ cup
	8x1 inch	1½ cups
	9x 1⅜ inches	4 cups
SOUFFLE PANS	various sizes	6 cups
SPRINGFORM PAN	8x3 inches	12 cups
	9x3 inches	16 cups

FRUIT, NUT & VEGETABLE EQUIVALENTS

Apples	3 medium = 1 lb. = 3 cups sliced
Beans, black & kidney	1 cup dry = $\frac{1}{2}$ lb. = $2\frac{1}{2}$ cups cooked
Beans, lima	$1\frac{1}{4}$ cup dry = $\frac{1}{2}$ lb. = 3 cups cooked
Beans, navy	1 cup dry = $\frac{1}{2}$ lb. = $2\frac{1}{2}$ cups cooked
Beets	1 lb. = 2 cups sliced
Broccoli	1 lb. head = 2 cups flowerets
Cauliflower	$1\frac{1}{2}$ lb. head = 2 cups cooked
Carrots	1 lb. = 3 cups shredded = $2\frac{1}{2}$ cups diced
Celery	1 large rib = $\frac{3}{4}$ cup diced
Cheese, soft	4 oz. = 1 cup shredded
Cheese, hard	3 oz. = 1 cup shredded
Chocolate, baking	1 square = 1 oz.
Chocolate chips	1 cup = 6 oz.
Corn	10 oz. = 2 cups
Frozen Vegetables	1 lb. = 3 cups
Garlic	3 large cloves = 1 tablespoon minced
Green beans, fresh	1 lb. = 3 cups fresh = $2\frac{1}{2}$ cups cooked
Herbs	1 teaspoon dry = 3 teaspoons fresh
Lemon	1 whole = 3 tablespoons juice = 2 teaspoons peel
Lime	1 whole = 2 tablespoon juice = $1\frac{1}{2}$ teaspoons peel
Mushrooms, fresh	1 lb. = 6 cups sliced = 4 cups chopped = 3 oz. dried
Onions	1 lb. = 3 large
Onions	1 large = 1 cup, chopped
Peanuts	1 lb. shelled = 4 cups
Pears	1 medium = 4 oz. = $\frac{1}{2}$ cup sliced
Pecans	1 cup = $3\frac{1}{2}$ oz. halves = 4 oz. chopped
Peppers, bell	1 large = 6 oz. = 1 cup diced
Potatoes	3 medium = 1 lb.
Rice, white	1 cup raw = 3 cups cooked
Rice, brown	1 cup raw = $3\frac{1}{8}$ cups cooked
Rice, wild	1 cup raw = 4 cups cooked
Spinach	1 lb. fresh = 6 cups leaves = $1\frac{3}{4}$ cups cooked
Squash, winter	1 lb. = 1 cup mashed
Tomato paste/sauce	8 oz. = 1 cup
Walnuts, halves	$3\frac{1}{2}$ oz. = 1 cup
Yeast	1 pkg. = 1 tablespoon = $\frac{1}{4}$ oz.
Zucchini	1 lb. = 3 cups sliced = $2\frac{1}{2}$ cups chopped

TEMPERATURE CONVERSIONS

Farenheit to Celsius:
subtract 32 and multiply by 0.5556.

Celsius to Farenheit:
add 32 and multiply by 18.

-10°F	-23°C (freezer storage)
0°F	-17.7°C
32°F	0°C (water freezes)
50°F	10°C
68°F	20°C (room temperature)
100°F	37.7°C
150°F	65.5°C
205°F	96.1°C (water simmers)
212°F	100°C (water boils)
300°F	148.8°C
325°F	162.8°C
350°F	177°C (baking)
375°F	190.5°C
400°F	204.4°C (hot oven)
425°F	218.3°C
450°F	232°C (very hot oven)
475°F	246.1°C
500°F	260°C (broiling)

MEASURING DRINKS

MEASUREMENT	EQUIVALENT
1 dash	6 drips
2 tablespoons	1 oz.
1 pony	1 oz.
1 finger	1 oz.
1 jibber	1½ - 2 oz.

CAN SIZES

CAN SIZE	AVERAGE WEIGHT OF CONTENTS	APPROXIMATE CUPFULS
No. ¼	4 oz.	½ cup
No. ½	8 oz.	1 cup
No. 1 tall	10.5 oz.	1¼ cups
No. 300	14 – 16 oz.	1¾ - 2 cups
No. 303	16 – 17 oz.	2 cups
No. 2	20 oz.	2½ cups
No. 2.5	29 oz.	3½ cups
No. 3	46 oz.	5¾ cups
No. 10	106 oz.	13 cups

EGG GRADES AND SIZES

GRADES
U.S. Grade AA (Fancy Fresh Quality)
U.S. Grade A

SIZE	PER DOZEN
Jumbo	30 oz.+
Extra Large	27 to 30 oz.
Large	24 to 27 oz.
Medium	21 to 24 oz.
Small	18 to 21 oz.

RECIPES AND NOTES

RECIPES AND NOTES